MW00768300

Bulletproof Putting

in Five Easy Lessons

The Streamlined System for Weekend Golfers

Michael McTeigue

Illustrations by David Wenzel

Also by Michael McTeigue

"The Keys to the Effortless Golf Swing"
Curing Your Hit Impulse in Seven Simple Lessons

ISBN 13: 978-1500848620 (CreateSpace Assigned)

For every golfer who was ever spooked
by a three-foot putt.

With Love
to Linda, Mindy, & Melody

With special appreciation
to Ken Bowden

Foreword

I was familiar with Mike McTeigue's teaching because I had read his 1985 book *The Keys to the Effortless Swing* during the time I was the Senior Instruction Editor at GOLF Magazine. It was a groundbreaking book in many ways and it had caught my attention.

The first time I actually met Mike McTeigue was when I had flown out from New York to his home base in Silicon Valley to work on an article with him for GOLF Magazine. I knew Mike was a very smart guy based on the conversations we had already had and the information we had exchanged about an idea he had brought to us that we were considering turning into a cover story.

I drove from the San Francisco airport to Mike's office in Sunnyvale and as I pulled into the parking lot, there were four geeky looking men in the parking lot driving a remote controlled mini-vehicle over a pile of rocks off to the side of the driveway. I stopped and asked them what they were doing. The response: "We're testing some new wheels for the Mars Rover." Mike hadn't told me his offices were located inside a NASA test center. At that point I knew this wasn't going to be a typical golf instruction article, and it wasn't.

We spent the day together and it was literally and figuratively as close to rocket science as I ever got writing golf instruction. It was clear that Mike was thinking about the swing and game at a much higher level than most of us in the industry. The result of that trip was one of the most interesting full swing articles GOLF Magazine ever had the pleasure of publishing and it actually turned into a series of articles that ran for several months after the cover story because we couldn't fit it all into a single story.

That GOLF Magazine series was published nearly two decades ago, so after all this time, I was very excited to see what Mike had put together for his latest golf book. Once again, his ability to break down, examine, and reassemble any complexity in the game is on full display in Bulletproof Putting.

In this beautifully illustrated volume, he has blended a deep understanding of statistical analysis, the art and science of reading greens, the biomechanics for creating a repeating stroke, the mindset of great putters and the keys to efficient practice into an easy to understand package.

I can't wait to see what his next project will be, but Mike, please don't wait another 30 years!

Lorin Anderson
President, Proponent Group

Contents

Introduction

"The man who can putt is a match for anyone."
-Willie Park Jr.

Did you ever walk off a green feeling like you had just been shot full of holes? You hit a superb approach shot eight feet above the hole. Your birdie putt caught a piece of the cup but spun three feet by. Then you left the three-footer SHORT OF THE CUP, turning a makeable birdie into a pitiful bogey. Or maybe, on a tough par four, you hit a sweet mid-iron shot thirty-five feet from the hole for a nice par opportunity. Unfortunately, you left the first putt waaaaay short, then – mad at yourself – blew the second putt four feet past, and - no, don't say it! - missed the lousy four footer, turning a probable par into a nasty double bogey.

We've all been there. Setbacks like these on the putting green can blow up a decent round and leave us shaking our heads and muttering in disgust as we head to the next tee. On the next green, even a simple two-foot tap-in provokes dread. If you've endured experiences like these and want to avoid them forevermore, the Bulletproof Putting System (BPS) is for you.

Why is my putting system called *bulletproof*? Because it protects you much like bulletproof vests protect SWAT teams. You might take some hits, but you won't get whacked on the greens. You won't see your putting fall apart and your game spin out of control. Your bulletproof system will minimize the damage and keep your head in the game.

One vital secret of the Bulletproof Putting System is it reduces the chances for FUD – fear, uncertainty, and doubt – to take control. It protects you from debilitating negative thoughts that creep in uninvited and cause an easy putt to become pure mental anguish. You'll feel secure in the confidence that you are a good putter and you have a system that works for you. You'll even enjoy the chance to apply it to those tricky three and four foot putts that aggravate all of us.

This system is *streamlined* for the *weekend golfer*. I am assuming you don't devote countless hours to practicing and playing, and that you're not interested in investigating the analytical complexities and subtle nuances of manipulating the flat stick. You simply want to sink more putts while feeling confident on the greens, right? If you typically are taking thirty-five or more putts per eighteen holes, the Bulletproof Putting System can help you consistently save five shots or more per round. Wouldn't you like to lower your average score by five shots this season? In this little book, I offer you a simple, precise system that you can choose to use exactly as prescribed, but you also can modify many elements to suit your personal preferences. When something is "highly-recommended," I call it out clearly.

Who Cares About Putting?

The next section introduces the elements of the bulletproof system, and subsequent lessons present each of them in detail. But first, let's look at a few reasons why you can benefit greatly from embracing the BPS and improving your putting, instead of spending nearly all of your precious practice time beating balls with your full swing.

Consider these observations:

- Putting comprises at least *forty percent* of your shots and maybe more.
- A two-inch putt counts as much as a 300-yard drive.
- The miniscule "leave" on a putt you should have made is as painful as a penalty stroke for a ball lost in a hazard, and it is the easiest penalty to avoid.
- The putt is the least complicated shot to execute, requiring the least athletic ability of all golf shots. Almost anyone can develop a bulletproof putting game just by focusing on a few simple concepts and techniques.
- The fastest way to lower your scores is to improve your putting. It is supremely difficult to improve your long game enough to hit five more greens in regulation per round, but it is quite feasible for the weekend golfer to take at least five fewer putts in eighteen holes.

- Good putting builds positive momentum. Finishing a hole by sinking a good putt gives you a boost of confidence that carries you to the next tee – and next green – in a positive frame of mind. It also can unnerve and demoralize your opponents to watch your bulletproof putting hole after hole.

The Bulletproof Putting System (BPS)

The BPS is a sensible system for increasing one-putts and reducing three-putts. It focuses on two primary goals: 1) sinking more putts of eight feet or less, and 2) lagging longer putts into your Slam Dunk Zone to avoid three putting. To achieve these goals consistently, we'll do the following:

- Build a simple, repeatable, dependable putting stroke
- Develop curiosity and imagination about "roll-path"
- Ingrain your bulletproof pre-shot and in-shot routines
- Learn strategies for the four types of putts: slam dunk, drillable, drainable, and lag
- Utilize precious practice and warm up time to your best advantage.

What the BPS system is NOT

The BPS is not a complicated treatise with a detailed analysis of every subtle and potential element of putting. Dave Pelz does an impressive job of that in his 394-page seminal work, *Dave Pelz's Putting Bible*, while Golf Magazine offers a mind-boggling compendium in *The Best Putting Instruction Book Ever*. As a weekend golfer, you probably don't have time for that, and there is a risk that too much information will overwhelm you.

The BPS is not the ONLY WAY to putt. I am sure one can find expert teachers and players who disagree with virtually everything I say in this book. They will point to great putters who violate every principal of the BPS. This is because there are countless ways to putt well. In fact, there are almost no universal putting fundamentals. Players have achieved fantastic results with wildly unorthodox styles. As just one example, the great Bobby Locke – once the hottest putter in professional golf – reportedly swung his putter across his target line with a slightly closed clubface, in blatant defiance of the bedrock fundamental that the face and path should be "square" to the target-line at impact.

My primary goal is to simplify this deceptively complex subject and offer you a concise, coherent method, a distilled set of strategies and techniques that lead to consistently better putting. These suggestions are starting points, which you are free to customize to suit your preferences. The main point is to commit *your definite approach* to all the elements of the system and then to stick with each of them. Ingrain them, make them reflexive. Change them very reluctantly.

Finally, the BPS is not an instantaneous fix. While it does contain some useful tips that might help you immediately, the important elements of the system must be refined by you over time. Even if you follow the program with enthusiasm, you might putt worse for the first couple of rounds because your mind will be occupied with new ways of thinking. It takes some time to make these changes habitual, especially the pre-shot and in-shot routines. You will be training your mind to perform a pre-determined sequence of events for twenty to forty seconds at a time. Believe it or not, this takes practice! If you apply the lessons of the BPS in the order presented, you'll minimize the annoyances of this transition period. I predict you'll follow two or three rounds of mediocre putting with a breakthrough round where you drain a bunch of putts and shoot far below your typical score, for your first taste of Bulletproof Putting. That will be your *AH-HA!* moment on your path to consistently better putting.

Let's get started!

Lesson 1 - Your Bulletproof Putting Stroke

"Putting is an entirely personal sort of thing and I believe it should be your own. There is really no right or wrong way to stand or set up. If you follow the sport, you know there have been many successful putters with radically different methods."

-Ben Crenshaw

The great putters of golf history agree: there are few, if any, absolutely essential stance and stroke mechanics. The simple goal of moving the putter head into the ball at the appropriate speed and on-line to the target can be achieved through a myriad of idiosyncratic styles. In fact, The BPS approach to putting mechanics requires only one essential element: keeping the putter face square to the target and moving, at an appropriate speed, toward the target for several inches through the ball position. Our Lesson 1 goal is to *develop a putting style you trust to make a repeatable stroke along a precise path several inches long.*

In this lesson, we cover the fundamentals of one simple, (mostly) mainstream putting stance and stroke that I believe you can master quickly. You are free to customize most of the elements to suit your personal taste. By embracing the concepts in this lesson, you will become very confident in your ability to roll your putts on your chosen line. In subsequent lessons, we will apply your bulletproof stroke to our four different types of putts and a variety of conditions.

If you have studied different approaches to putting mechanics, you probably will agree that most fall into one of two general buckets: "arc putters" versus "pendulum putters." In a nutshell, arc putters keep the putter relatively low to the ground as they swing it in a horizontal arc that aligns precisely with the target line only in the instant the putter strikes the ball. Pendulum putters, in contrast, strive to keep the putter moving straight along the target line as long as possible on either side of the ball, which requires the putter to move a bit more up and down during the stroke.

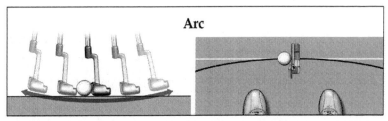

Arc Stroke: The putter head's vertical arc moves more parallel to the ground, but its horizontal arc moves along the target line only briefly.

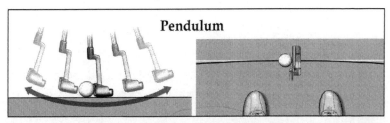

The Pendulum Stroke: The putter head's vertical arc moves more up and down, while its horizontal arc moves along the target line for several inches on each side of the ball.

There are many vocal advocates of each approach, and they cite legendary putters who use their method. It is in vogue these days to recommend the arc stroke created by a miniscule, lateral rotation of the shoulders. This is a fine approach for talented athletes and skilled players who devote adequate time to grooving a stroke that hits the ball in the exact instant the putter face aligns to the target. In the Bulletproof Putting System, I recommend the **pendulum stroke** for the weekend golfer because I believe it is far easier to keep the putter face aligned to the target through impact, and it can be mastered with a minimal amount of practice.

The mechanics of the bulletproof putting stroke have these important elements:

- A shoulder-controlled pendulum stroke along the target line through the impact zone
- Eyes directly above the target line
- Hands directly below the shoulders
- Good stroke rhythm
- Follow-through longer than backswing.

These simple mechanics can be learned and ingrained with ease. There are plenty of other elements to consider about stance and stroke – and we'll discuss many of them – but everything else is customizable to suit your personal preferences.

Our key idea is this: you can easily develop a dependable putting stroke that rolls the ball consistently along the target line you select. The more complex and nuanced subject of picking the right target line will entertain us in the next lesson. For now, let's streamline your putting stroke.

The Grip

I shall offer only a few simple suggestions about placing your hands on the putter grip. I have lost track of all the different types of putting grips: overlap, reverse overlap, split hands, cross-handed, claw, box, etc. Most of them are designed to keep the right hand from being too active during the stroke, and I recommend them only if your right hand insists on manipulating the putter. For now, let's use the traditional *reverse overlapping grip.*

If you are a right handed player, place your left hand on the putter grip in its usual position, but with your thumb directly on top of the shaft. Place your right hand below the left, with the right thumb on top of the shaft, as well. The shaft should run more vertically up your palms than it does for your shot making grip.

Your palms should be facing each other, with your right palm aligned with the putter face. This is an important suggestion because properly aiming the putter face is more important than stroking the putter head on line. Soon you will develop a repeatable stroke that moves the club head on a predictable path, and it is critically important that the clubface is aligned with the path of the stroke. The easiest way to achieve this alignment is to let your palms face each other, while making certain your right palm is aligned with the putter face.

Link your hands by lifting the left index finger and wrapping it over the fingers of your right hand. This is the classic reverse overlapping putter grip used by the majority of good players. That said, if you have a different grip you like, and that aligns the putter face to the path, keep it!

The vitally important element of the grip is this: *the hands do not manipulate the club in any way during the bulletproof putting stroke.* (I realize it is trendy these days to speak of "releasing the putter," but it is an unnecessary concept in bulletproof putting.) The hands connect the club to the arms and shoulders. Think of the forearms and club forming a letter Y. We will use the shoulders to move the Y and make a repeatable "teeter-totter" stroke. The Y must never change shape during the putting motion, especially at the junction between the arms and the club, i.e. the grip.

Just to be clear, the bulletproof putting stroke for the weekend golfer is *NOT* wristy. The wrists do not hinge or flex or rotate during the stroke; the hands do not push the handle; and the bottom of the Y does not waggle independently at any time.

This is not to imply that wristy putters don't make a lot of putts; there have been many great wristy putters, including Arnold Palmer, Billy Casper, Bobby Locke, and Bobby Jones. A wristy stroke is more complicated, requires more finesse, and, when misused, can pull the putter head off-line to the left and decelerate the club head through impact. Let's leave wrist action for players who want to spend a lot more time on the practice green refining their strokes. The weekend golfer does not need to worry about how and when to engage his/her wrists on a putt.

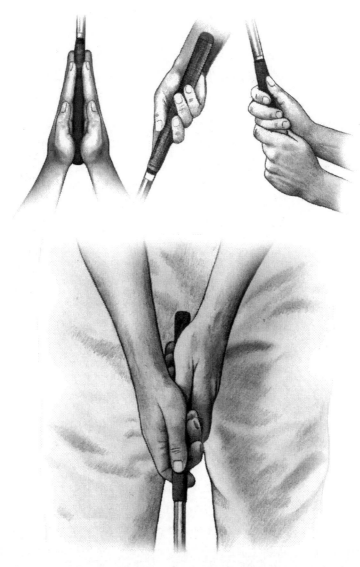

Reverse Overlapping Putting Grip: Align your palms to each other and to the putter face. Run the putter grip vertically up your palms. Place your thumbs vertically on top of the grip. Extend your left index finger over one to three fingers of your right hand.

So, grip the putter any way that feels most comfortable to you and forms a stable Y attaching your arms to the club, with your right palm aligned with the putter face.

Grip *pressure* is another easy topic. Some years ago, Lew Fishman of Golf Digest and I conducted a study that measured tour players' grip pressure while putting. Most held their putters at less than twenty percent of their maximum possible grip pressure, and they kept the pressure surprisingly constant throughout their strokes. I suggest the weekend golfer apply the *minimum pressure needed to maintain the shape and structure* of the Y during the stroke and keep that pressure as steady as possible during the stroke. Now, some teachers advise lighter grip pressure on short putts and more pressure on longer putts. Others suggest the exact opposite! Let us keep it simple and maintain consistent, light grip pressure sufficient to form a structurally stable, one-piece Y made by the forearms and club.

Generating the Stroke Motion

So far, the arms and club are molded together by an immovable (but not tense or tight) grip to form a Y, which is attached to the shoulders. We move the Y to swing the putter. How exactly shall we move the Y during the putting stroke?

We immobilize the shoulder *joints* (as we did with the wrist joints) and thereby make the arms and club dependent on the rocking of the shoulders at a pivot point on the top of the spine, to move the Y along the desired path. In essence, we are placing a connecting brace or "top" on the Y and using a slight, teeter-totter motion to rock the shoulders up and down and move the Y in a pendulum motion. Perhaps this sounds more complicated than simply whacking the ball with the wrists or swinging the Y from the unlocked shoulder joints (or some combination of the two), yet I believe it is an easier motion to repeat reliably without a lot of practice – which, of course, makes it ideal for the weekend golfer.

Let's get a feel for this motion. Stand up straight, point the Y straight out in front of you, and let your upper arms rest on the sides of your rib cage. Feel the pointy bone in the inside of each elbow joint press lightly into your torso, essentially securing your upper arms to your torso. Rotate your torso (and shoulders) ever so slightly to move the Y in a horizontal arc.

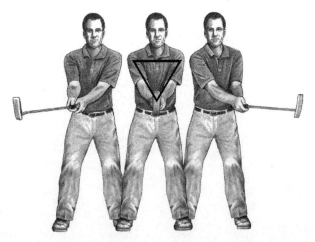

To feel the source of movement in the pendulum stroke, move the Y made by your arms and club in a lateral arc by gently rotating the upper torso.

How does that feel? Now, tilt your spine to drop the putter head down, close to the ground, and repeat the motion. Place the putter head along your visible line on a tile, rug, or floorboard. Can you swing the Y to move the putter head along the line on the floor by moving your shoulders up and down slightly, in a teeter-totter motion?

An easy way to highlight the feeling is to place the shaft of a different golf club across your chest and under each arm just above the elbows. As you make the up-and-down, teeter-totter motion with your shoulders, the two ends of the club shaft should move clearly up and down (and never around). How does this feel?

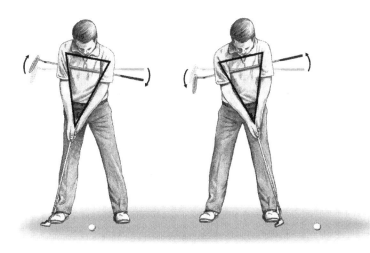

Place a second club under your armpits and across your chest. Move the ends of the club vertically up and down with a teeter-totter motion of your shoulders.

If you read golf magazines or golf instruction books and blogs, you probably will discover other stroking motions of higher complexity. You might find a combination arm and wrist motion, including "release" at impact, or elbow putters, or arm/shoulder putters with dual fulcrums. There are fabulous putters who use more complex motions than the one I am recommending for weekend golfers, yet there also are countless outstanding putters who use the simple, teeter-totter, shoulder stroke of the stabilized Y.

The Bulletproof Putting Stance

I am tempted to say I don't care how you set up to the putt (i.e., assume your stance), but that is not quite true. If you adopt the pendulum shoulder stroke I recommend, you will benefit from specific set up techniques. They are not complicated, and we will put them all together in a concise routine in the lesson on establishing your bulletproof pre-shot and in-shot routines. For now, let's list them and discuss the rationale for them.

An important and necessary term we'll refer to often in putting is the *target line*. For our purposes, the target line is a specific, imaginary line on which the ball sits. This line extends from the ball to the target we want the ball to begin rolling toward (not necessarily the hole, as we will discuss later). The target line defines the ball's initial roll path and, therefore, the path of the putter head during the stroke. The target line also extends from the ball in the opposite direction of the target for at least a foot or two (I'll say *downline* when I refer to the part of the target line which is behind the ball and runs away from the target.).

To help establish your set up, find a full length mirror and stand with the mirror to your downline side (right side if you are a righty). Place a ball on the ground and perhaps add another club shaft, ruler, or piece of string directly behind the ball to represent a target line running perpendicular to the mirror and directly away from it.

Grip the club and form your Y while standing erect, as we did in the previous section. Let your upper arms rest against the sides of your ribs. Now bend from the hips until your putter head is behind a golf ball on the floor. Turn your head to the downline side to look into the mirror. Arrange yourself to achieve two vital positions, while keeping the putter head directly behind the ball.

First, make sure *your eyes are directly over the target line, an inch or so downline from the ball.* As you swivel your head to look over the ball, along the target line to your target, your eyes should be aligned directly above the target line. If you dangle a club shaft or yardstick down from a point between your eyes at the top of your nose, it must point to a spot directly on the target line, slightly behind the ball. This is non-negotiable, because it will help to ensure you are actually aiming at your target.

If your eyes are not over the target line, your aiming will be faulty: you will mistakenly aim to the left of your actual target if your eyes are past/outside the target line, and you will mistakenly aim to the right of your target if your eyes are short of/inside the target line. Sure, a player with great talent and intuition can compensate successfully – and some tour players with arc strokes do place their eyes an inch or two inside the target line – but why complicate things needlessly?

The second vital position (again looking in the downline mirror) is to *hang your hands directly under a line connecting your shoulders,* so the plane formed by your shoulders and hands is vertical to the ground.

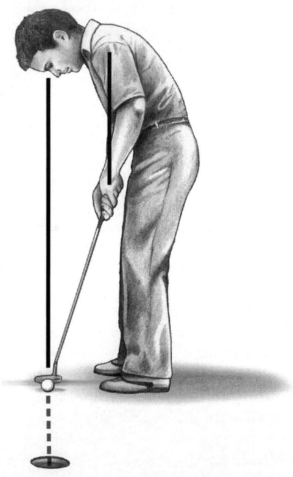

Position your eyes directly over the target line and your hands directly under your shoulder joints to improve the accuracy and consistency of your stroke.

Why? Because this alignment generates a straighter stroke when you make the teeter-totter motion with your shoulders. The putter will move along a straight line through the ball very reliably. If your hands are farther away from your body, your stroke will move in a concave arc. If your hands are closer to your body, your stroke will move in a convex arc. In both cases, the putter will move off the target line to a greater extent.

These two fundamentals – eyes over the target line, and hands directly below the line connecting the shoulders – will influence other elements of the stance, such as how far you stand from the ball, how much you bend at the hips, how far down you place your hands on your putter, and even the ideal angle of your putter shaft relative to the putter head.

Different body types will require different postures and perhaps different length putters to comfortably achieve these two fundamental positions. For instance, a player with a long torso and relatively short arms will stand farther away from the ball and use a longer putter than a player with a short torso and long arms. Please experiment a bit with this until you find a comfortable position, because once you find it you'll be ready to make your bulletproof stroke.

All things being equal, I prefer you to bend over quite a bit from the hips – while still keeping eyes over the ball and hands directly below the shoulders. The rationale is simple: the more you bend over, the more your shoulders rise and fall on a vertical plane and the longer your putter stays on the target line during the stroke. An acceptable alternative, especially for players with long torsos, is to bend less from the hips while curving the top of the spine more.

Curve your spine or bend from the hips to get your eyes, shoulders, and hands well-positioned for your teeter-totter/pendulum stroke.

Experiment in the mirror until you can achieve the two fundamentals of the stance and, when you make a pendulum stroke with your shoulders, your putter moves directly along the target line for four or five inches on either side of the ball.

Questions typically arise about alignment of the body relative to the target line. Should you align your feet and shoulders parallel to the target line, or should you pull your target-side foot back to give you a better look at the target? Good players exhibit many variations in alignment, but most select their preferred alignment and stick with it. My strong recommendation for bulletproof putting with a pendulum stroke is to align your feet and shoulders parallel to the target line – what we call **square to the target line**.

Your shoulders must be square to the target line in order to keep the putter moving on the target line during the pendulum stroke. If your shoulders are aligned to the left of the target line (called **open**), your pendulum stroke will tend to miss your putts to the left. Since your shoulders are square, you might as well line your elbows, hips, and feet up squarely, too.

Experiment with alignment. Place your putter head over a ruler, board, or line in your carpet; assume your stance with eyes over the target line and hands under your shoulders; and make a few teeter-totter strokes over the line with your shoulders. Try changing your foot position and aligning your shoulders to the right or left a bit. What happens? A true pendulum stroke from the shoulders will remain aligned with the shoulders and move in the direction you change your alignment. For example, if you **opened** your feet and shoulders, your putter path probably will be left of the target.

Refining the Bulletproof Stroke

You now have the basics in place to make a repeatable putting stroke.

- You form a stable, one-piece Y with your forearms and club.

- You align your eyes over the target line.
- You hang your hands directly below your shoulder line.

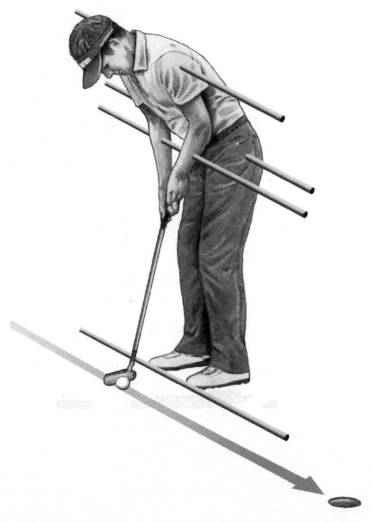

Aligning your feet, hips, elbows, and shoulders parallel to the target line makes it easier to keep your stroke on line.

- You align your feet, hips, and shoulders parallel to your target line.
- You make a teeter-totter, pendulum motion of the Y by moving the shoulders up and down.
- You perform this motion to stroke the putter straight along a line on the floor with reassuring consistency.

It is not difficult, is it? If you are experiencing difficulty making a nice straight stroke for four to five inches on either side of the ball position, please review the previous section and experiment a bit more in the mirror. Be sure your hands are directly below your shoulders and you have enough forward bending or spinal curve to let the shoulders teeter-totter on a vertical plane. We do not want or need to over-think the bulletproof putting stroke. The best way to refine it is simply to practice your stroke while suspending the putter head over a ruler or a line on the floor.

If the putter head swings in a bit of an arc at each end of a longer putting stroke, this is nothing to worry about. It is unavoidable, unless your spine is parallel to the ground. However, we only care about the putter's path for a few inches on either side of the ball, and you should be able to master this easily. If you keep the putter moving directly over the line for four to five inches on each side of the ball, you are doing fine.

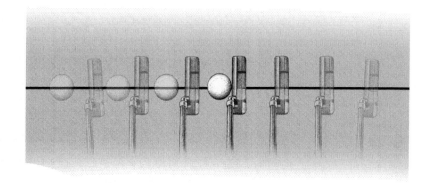

A primary objective of bulletproof putting is to stroke the putter on a straight line for four or five inches on either side of the ball.

Now we will cover the two remaining elements of the bulletproof stroke: its rhythm and its length. To a considerable degree, rhythm influences stroke length, so we will explore that factor first. Stroke **rhythm** refers to the relative speeds the putter head moves during the stroke. Bulletproof rhythm is subtle, never abrupt. Because the movement stems from the shoulders, not the hands, the backswing pace is moderate, even slow. Because the muscles moving the club back (in the "teeter") are big muscles of the torso, they require an instant of time to release their contraction, while opposing muscles begin contracting to move the putter toward the ball and target. For this reason, the change of direction should be slow, casual, and never rushed.

In the Bulletproof Putting System, *the primary reason for ruined putts is rushing the change-of-direction during the stroke.* A momentary pause at the top of the back stroke is highly desirable because it reduces the chances of a handsy push or a jerky twitch of the chest muscles.

Likewise, once the forward motion (the "totter") has been initiated by the dropping of the downline shoulder, the acceleration of the club builds gradually, even subtly. The forward motion is a smooth stroke to the finish, not a push, slap, or pop. Maintaining constant grip pressure helps to ensure a smooth forward stroke controlled by the dropping of the downline shoulder.

I have a favorite image I use to help me pause momentarily at the change-of-direction and allow my pendulum motion to proceed smoothly on the forward stroke. I imagine a long, thick rubber band attached to my target on one end and to the bottom part of my putter shaft on the other. As I make my teeter motion on the backswing, I feel the imaginary rubber band stretch.

As I finish the backswing, I pause briefly – as one would with a slingshot – then I allow the rubber band to "pull" the putter forward to the hole. This forward totter motion feels like a response to the pulling of the rubber band. The putter shaft is being pulled, rather than pushed, through the ball toward the target.

This rubber band image has added benefits: it helps me calibrate the length of the stroke to fit the distance I want to roll the ball, and it keeps me focused on following through to my target. I hope you find it as useful as I do.

Stretching and releasing an imaginary rubber band during the stroke helps to create good stroke rhythm.

To summarize rhythm of the putting stroke, we allow the movement of the big muscles of the torso to control the relative speeds. The backstroke is unhurried; there is a slight pause; and the forward stroke is unhurried. Acceleration on the forward stroke is gradual and subtle.

The subject of rhythm naturally leads to consideration of **tempo**, the overall speed of the stroke. Instructors often say your swing tempo should mirror your personality; hyper players will have a fast tempo and laid back folks will prefer an unhurried tempo. There may be truth to this, which is fine; however, a more potent influence on tempo is the type of putting stroke deployed. The shoulder-based pendulum stroke will require a slower tempo than a handsy or wristy stroke because big muscles in the torso are firing to make the stroke. Your tempo should be determined by the speed at which your torso muscles contract and release in sequence, maintaining good rhythm. I do believe younger players typically can execute the bulletproof stroke at a faster tempo than senior players because their muscles fire faster.

Whatever your natural tempo, it is best to maintain it on all your putts. Don't deliberately try to swing faster or slower on putts of different lengths; that will take care of itself. In truth, the time required to stroke a five foot putt will be nearly identical to the time required to stroke a thirty foot putt, but that will happen automatically when you stroke your putts with good rhythm.

The final of our five elements of bulletproof putting mechanics involves the *length* of your putting stroke. Because we strive for a consistent rhythm and tempo, we must use the length of the backswing and follow-through to influence how far we roll the ball. Here are a few simple guidelines. The length of the backswing varies with the length of the putt. In general, you want to use the minimum backswing length needed to roll the ball the desired distance, while maintaining good rhythm and tempo in the stroke. Too long a backswing typically leads to deceleration on the forward swing, while too short a backswing usually causes the player to slap at or pop the ball with a handsy motion. If you practice good rhythm and consistent tempo, you consistently will make the appropriate backswing motion.

A simple, rule-of-thumb formula for determining length of the backstroke is one inch of backswing for each one foot of putt distance. For example, make a six-inch backswing for a six-foot putt. Naturally, this will vary depending on the slope and speed of the green. Use this formula as a mere guideline, and please don't get hung up trying to measure and control your backswing distance precisely. The key is to lengthen your stroke for longer putts, while maintaining your bulletproof tempo and rhythm.

The most important element of the bulletproof stroke is to keep the putter head moving along the target line for at least several inches past the ball. This simple act will compensate for a host of small deficiencies, especially on short putts.

The follow-through stroke (past the ball position) should usually be longer than the backswing. This helps to ensure you accelerate gradually through the ball. A good, general ratio is one-third backswing, two-thirds follow-through, that is, a follow-through twice as long as your backswing.

That said, the backswing/follow-through ratio varies depending on length of putt. On short putts, the ratio might be one part backswing and four parts follow-through. On long putts of twenty feet or more, the lengths of the backswing and the follow-through might be nearly equal. On putts of eight to ten feet, the one-third backswing, two-thirds follow-through ratio applies nicely. There is no need to obsess about this; it will happen naturally as you progress through this book. For now, just endeavor to make your follow-through stroke longer than your backswing stroke.

Aiming

It is well understood that aiming the putter face correctly is more important than stroking the putter along the proper line. When there is a discrepancy between the face aim and the line of the stroke, the ball will begin to move on a line about seventy percent closer to the face aim than the stroke path! In practical terms, if you aim the face incorrectly, but stroke the putter along the correct path, you are likely to miss the putt. If you aim the face correctly, but your stroke is a bit off, you still might make the putt.

Our goal, of course, is to aim the putter correctly and then to swing the putter along the line to which the face is aligned. We want zero discrepancy between face aim and swing path. So, how can you assure your face aim is correct?

Believe it or not, there is no simple answer. Tests have shown that most players align properly from some distances but not others with a given putter, and different styles of putters increase the likelihood of misalignment to the right or left. To deal with these challenges, I have experimented with various alignment training aids over the years and found that most have limitations.

I prefer laser beams that align with the face and shine a beam along a line perpendicular to the putter face, especially when the user can line up the putter, then activate the laser to see where the face is aiming. Unfortunately, ensuring the beam is aligned (calibrated) correctly is a challenge; the laser is difficult to secure properly; and the weight of the laser throws the putter out of balance. If you discover a good, durable, laser training device for putting, please let me know! The best laser device I have seen currently on the market is Dave Pelz's *Lazr Aimer*. It is not inexpensive, but it is well-designed and effective.

There are a few simple ways to improve your likelihood of aiming correctly.

- First, as mentioned above, be sure your eyes are directly over the target line.
- Second, align your palms to each other and the putter face when you assume your grip.
- Third, use a putter with a definite alignment guide (see illustration below).
- Fourth, use a *golf ball alignment marker* to draw a straight line on your ball, and point the line at your target from behind the ball, as part of your pre-shot routine. When you take your stance, you align your putter's alignment guide to the line on your ball, and chances are improved you will aim properly.
- Fifth, I have found it highly useful to practice with a *putting matt* that has alignment guides on it. Yes, the alignment guides on the matt are a "crutch," but experience has convinced me the training is effective.

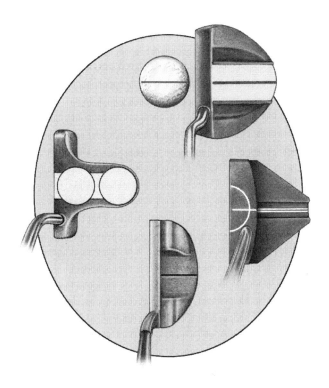

A putter with a good alignment guide will improve your aim and help you sink more putts. Align the guide to a straight line drawn on the circumference of your ball.

I wish I had an easy solution to the challenge of aiming the putter. If you are technically oriented, you can deep dive on the topic by reading *See It and Sink It* by Dr. Craig Farnsworth, a Denver optometrist who has helped some of the best putters in golf. For the weekend golfer, though, the most useful way to assess how well you align is to monitor whether you miss relatively straight five-foot putts consistently to the right or left. Assuming you practice making a repeatable stroke along a straight line for a few inches on each side of the ball, you will know you are aiming incorrectly if you miss consistently to the same side of the cup.

We now have the essential bulletproof putting mechanics in place. You should be able to repeat a shoulder-based pendulum stroke that tracks consistently over a line on the floor, with your eyes directly over that line. Leave a putter lying around the house and do a million of these strokes, both with and without a ball. Focus on aligning the face to the line and moving the putter along the line until you are absolutely confident you can repeat that stroke automatically, without thinking about it.

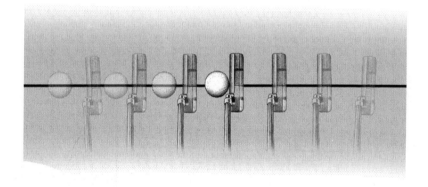

Practice at home a few minutes each day until you trust your pendulum stroke to move the putter on a straight line for four or five inches on either side of the ball.

In Lesson 3, we will aim at specific targets and start sinking putts.

Frequently Asked Questions

Before leaving our discussion of putting mechanics, let us consider some common questions. These topics are not core to bulletproof putting, yet they might help to remove any confusion about the how's and why's of the putting stroke. If you are comfortable with your bulletproof stance and stroke, you can skip this section and progress to the next lesson.

Where should I place the ball in my stance? Because your eyes are over the target line directly behind the ball, and the stem of your Y is aligned with the center of your body, your ball should be positioned approximately in line with a point between your target-side eye and ear. This position situates your eyes slightly behind the ball and allows your putter to strike the ball as it reaches the bottom of its vertical arc along the target line.

How far apart should I place my feet? This is up to you. Your stance should be wide enough to create stability, but not so wide you tend to sway during the stroke. Start with your feet positioned directly below your hip joints, and adjust from there for comfort. There should be no motion of the lower body during the stroke. Some players like to place the feet closer together on shorter putts and farther apart on longer putts. This helps them calibrate the length of their backswings. In his excellent book, *Putt to Win*, Dave Stockton advocates bowing your legs slightly at address to stabilize your body during the stroke.

How far should I stand from the ball? This is determined entirely by where you must place your feet to position your eyes over the target line and your hands under your shoulders. If you bend forward a lot, which has advantages, your feet naturally will move farther from the target line.

How much should I bend my arms? Let's be careful to not get carried away by over analysis. As you form your Y with your inner elbows touching your sides, your forearms will extend to the putter grip at about a 45 degree angle, much as they do in the letter Y. The exact degree of arm bend will vary, depending on your torso and arm length and your degree of bending from the hips. That said, as long as you can move your Y to swing your putter precisely along the target line, you can bend your arms as little or as much as you like. As you look down at your arms, an imaginary line connecting your elbows should align parallel to the target line, so one elbow is not higher than the other.

Is it OK to move my head during the stroke? In general, moving your head during the bulletproof stroke is a very bad idea. It rarely helps and usually hurts. If the muscles in your shoulders and neck are stiff or tight, you might see a tiny rocking of your nose and chin as you make the teeter-totter motion. This is no problem, so don't try to stop it. Nevertheless, you do not want the top of your spine moving laterally right or left or vertically up and down during the stroke. A steady pivot point at the top of your spine will stabilize your pendulum stroke and keep your putter moving straight over the target line.

Where should I look during the putting stroke?
Your eyes are extremely important as you read the putt
and prepare for the stroke, but they are largely irrelevant
once the stroke is underway. In fact, the eyes often cause
problems during the stroke, and you might discover you
actually putt quite well with your eyes closed as you
make your bulletproof stroke. As we will discuss in
Lesson 4 on establishing a putting routine, your mind
should be occupied with images of the ball rolling along
the path to the hole, not making visual observations of the
stroke as it happens.

Most importantly, you should NOT watch the putter
head moving back and forth during the putting stroke
(except when you are training yourself to swing along the
target line). Watching the putter head has two potential
problems. First, it increases the likelihood of swaying
your head away from and toward the target as your eyes
move to watch the putter head swing back and forward.
Second, as you watch the putter swing back, you are more
apt to have an errant, destructive thought such as, "Oops,
I took the putter back too far..." or "Shoot, I am swinging
offline..." Thoughts such as these usually ruin the putt.

You have to do something with your eyes during the
stroke, so here are three options to explore. All three
require you to keep your eyes fixed on a single spot for
the entire stroke. First, gaze casually at a spot on the top
of the ball or on the back of the ball where the putter will
make contact during the stroke. (If you are using a line on
the ball as an alignment guide, gaze at that line.) Some
players advocate creating an image of tapping a tack into
the back of the ball. The second option is to fix your gaze

on a blade of grass between the ball and the putter head, a method I believe Ben Crenshaw used with great success. This reduces the possibility of flinching slightly at impact. A third option is to pick a spot a couple inches in front of the ball, on the target line, and watch it until the putter reaches it in the follow-through. This feels odd at first, but some players – notably, Dave Stockton – swear by it.

For me, the easiest of the three options just mentioned is to gaze in a "soft" way at the top of the ball. Wherever you decide to fix your gaze, do your best to hold that gaze until the stroke is complete. Many potentially good putts are ruined when the player looks up too soon to watch the motion of the ball toward the target.

Should I strike the ball on the upstroke? Some players and teachers advocate "topping" putts – striking upward into the ball above its equator with the leading edge of the putter. They believe it contributes to a more consistent initial rolling of the ball by eliminating any skidding of a lofted putt. I have tried this from time to time, but don't see any big advantage. I prefer to keep the putter head moving parallel to the ground through the impact zone. However, you can experiment with this, using your bulletproof stroke, simply by aligning the ball a bit more toward the target on your set up, so your putter head is on its upward arc when it contacts the ball.

Do I need to hit the ball on the putter's sweetspot? Yes. The sweetspot is the area on the putter face that provides the most solid contact with the ball and sends it farther and straighter than off-center hits. Consistently hitting the sweetspot is important because it reduces variability, but it is more difficult than you might think. I advise the weekend golfer to use a putter with good perimeter weighting in the clubhead, which makes the sweetspot larger and more forgiving.

On super-fast greens, skilled players occasionally address the ball away from the sweet spot, near the toe of the putter, to dampen its force. Few weekend golfers play on greens requiring such an adjustment.

Should I make a forward press to start the stroke? A forward press is a slight movement, typically of the hands and putter grip, toward the target as a preliminary motion to ensure everything is in synch at the start of the backswing. Some players and teachers strongly advocate it in putting. I like it too, although I prefer a very slight, almost imperceptible forward press with the shoulder pendulum. A bigger forward press, one that moves the putter handle an inch or more toward the target, can cause problems: it can deloft the putter, move the putter face off line, cause a change in grip pressure, and/or put the hands in control of the stroke. You do not *need* a forward press with the pendulum stroke, and if you do decide to use it please keep it small.

I don't feel comfortable with the pendulum stroke; what else can you recommend? Let me be clear; it does not matter which method of stroking the putt you embrace, as long as it swings the well-aimed putter head along the target line for about five inches from impact into the follow-through. In fact, if you study the great putters in golf history, you'll be amazed at how strikingly different their methods were. I hesitate to discuss this, though, because I believe the shoulder pendulum stroke is the best bet for the weekend golfer. You don't have to practice and refine it all that much. If you set up in a square stance and teeter-totter your shoulders, good things happen.

However, if you really dislike the shoulder pendulum motion, please do experiment with different ways to stroke the putt. You might try a simple stroke dominated by forearm motion that Jack Nicklaus describes in his classic, *Golf My Way*. Your torso remains relatively still while your arms move from the shoulder joints. Assume the bulletproof stance, with your eyes over the target line and your hands aligned directly below your shoulders. While keeping your right (target side) elbow close to your side, rotate your left elbow out, away from your body a bit, so it can move freely from the shoulder joint. Lower your right shoulder and make sure your right palm is vertical to the ground and facing the target directly. Now, rock your right forearm back and forth in a piston motion to move your right palm and your putter along the target line. Your right arm supplies the power and your right hand determines the direction of the stroke. Your left forearm accommodates the right arm piston. It should be pretty easy to keep the club on the correct path; the challenge for the weekend golfer is controlling the rhythm of the stroke and the speed of the putt.

This is just one option. After you experiment with as many different approaches as you wish, it is advisable to pick one and commit to it for the current season, at a minimum.

What kind of putter should I use? That is up to you; it is all about what looks and feels good and gives you confidence. While some instructors make a handsome living fitting players for expensive custom putters, I believe there is no need to spend a fortune on a putter. Just find one that gives you confidence. When you are shopping for a putter, look for perimeter weighting, a balanced face, a good aiming guide, a comfortable weight, and appropriate length for your bulletproof stance and stroke. A mallet putter head might be slightly better than a blade for the pendulum-shoulder stroke. Again, these are guidelines, not requirements. If you love your old Bullseye blade putter with no aiming guide, that's fine with me.

Grip size is largely dependent on the size of your hands, but generally I recommend a fatter grip for the pendulum stroke, with a flat spot on top for the thumbs.

Isn't "feel" more important in putting than mechanics? My definitive answer: yes and no. *Feel* in this context refers to a mind-body anticipation and subtle kinesthetic sensation of how the putt should be stroked to achieve the desired result. It is the result of the mind's analysis of its observations about the factors likely to affect the roll path of the ball. Feel is critically important in judging break and speed and translating that judgment into the correct stroke line and length. Feel is also the most enjoyable aspect of putting. Most of the greatest putters in golf history – Nicklaus, Woods, Casper, Locke, Crenshaw, Jones, Stockton, Faxon, Lowe, to name a few – relied heavily on feel, and they shared few if any mechanics in common.

However, feel must be supported by sound stroke mechanics. First we build a reliable, repeatable mechanical motion along a predictable line, and then we trust our feel to synthesize and translate our analysis into a well-calibrated, bulletproof stroke. This lesson helps you to develop your bulletproof stroke mechanics. Subsequent lessons will enliven and engage your *feel* for putting.

Quick Review

As we complete this lesson on the bulletproof putting stroke, I hope you already feel you can stroke the putter consistently along the intended line with a comfortable rhythm. Recall there are only five important elements to master:

- A shoulder-controlled pendulum stroke along the target line. I recommend achieving this by forming a Y with the putter-shaft and your arms and anchoring it to the torso, which makes a teeter-totter motion centered at the top of the spine.
- Eyes directly above the target line, slightly behind the ball, to ensure you swing along the target line.
- Hands directly below the shoulders, ensuring a straighter stroke along the target line.
- Good stroke rhythm, allowing the big muscles of the torso to control the backswing and forward swing. Recall the rubber band image to encourage good rhythm.
- Follow-through longer than backswing on all putts, to keep the putter moving to the target. Lengthen the backswing for longer putts.

Jackie Burke, a world class putter, observed, "Bad putting stems from thinking *how* instead of *where*." We want you to move from the *how* to the *where* as soon as possible. I strongly encourage you to practice your bulletproof stroke for a few moments every day, until you firmly believe you can start your stroke and it will naturally swing the putter along your desired line, without any effort from you. Make your stroke reflexive, automatic. Once you have that certainty, you can focus all your attention on the path and speed of the ball as it makes its journey to the hole, which is the subject of our next lesson.

Lesson 2 –Roll Path Curiosity and Imagination

"Good putting starts with seeing the ball going into the hole before you take your stance – in fact, before you even take your putter in hand."

-Dave Stockton, *Dave Stockton's Putt to Win*

"I can truthfully say that I have holed very few putts when I could not see definitely the path the ball should follow into the hole."

-Bobby Jones, *Bobby Jones on Golf*

The second aspect of bulletproof putting is reading greens and committing – with an unconflicted mind – to the line each putt must travel into the hole. I call this imaginary line the **roll path**, similar to the flight path of full-swing golf shots. Although it never leaves the ground, roll path has many of the elements of flight path: distance, curve, and changes in elevation and speed. While flight path can be influenced by external variables such as wind, humidity, elevation, and temperature, roll path is affected primarily by the texture, length, and grain of the grass, by moisture, and by the changes in elevation and slope of the putting surface.

Path is an appropriate word, because roll paths are actually about four inches wide. We tend to believe we have to hit putts along lines thinner than strands of spaghetti, but the equator of the ball can be two inches off-line to either side and still drop into the hole.

Roll path is a battle between force, friction, and gravity. The force of your putting stroke imparts a certain amount of forward momentum to the ball, which is slowed by gravity and the friction of the grass and is pulled by gravity down side-hill slopes. Early in each battle, the forward momentum of the ball is stronger and the effects of gravity and friction appear relatively weaker. As continual friction slows the ball, the effect of gravity appears stronger. On a given slope, the ball will curve more as its speed slows. This means most of the curve, or **break**, in the putt will occur in the last part of its roll path, nearer the hole. The majority of putts have break in their roll paths, and the amount and rate of break varies considerably from putt to putt. We **read** greens to assess the likely effects of friction and gravity and to estimate and **feel** the amount of force we need to apply to the ball with the putter to create an appropriate roll path.

I strongly believe the ability to accurately read greens and predict roll paths is at least half the battle in putting. It is much more complex and challenging than aiming and stroking the ball onto the desired roll path.

To illustrate my point, consider this question. If you challenged the average tour player to hit putts on an eight foot practice putting rug on a perfectly flat floor, how many would you expect him to make out of 100 putts? Based on my personal experience, I'd predict the average tour player consistently would make more than 90 percent, and many would sink 100 in a row. Yet the average U.S. PGA tour player only sinks about half his eight foot putts during tournaments. Why is that? We might never know for sure, but I'll suggest that subtle variations in roll path are the major factor, surpassing even competitive pressure.

If predicting successful roll path on any given putt is that tricky even for tour players, what can the weekend golfer do to have a fighting chance? I have four suggestions, and I'll discuss each in turn:

- Be realistic about your chances.
- Stay highly curious about roll path and reading greens.
- Exercise your imagination.
- Be decisive.

After we cover these four topics, we'll combine your bulletproof stroke and your green reading abilities in Lesson 3, and we'll apply them in Lesson 4 to the four kinds of putts: slam dunks, drillable, drainable, and lag putts.

Be Realistic About Your Chances

It is natural to expect your putting to save your score. Putting, of course, occurs at the conclusion of the hole, when the score for that hole is determined by putting results. Most of us expect to convert eight, ten, twelve, and fifteen foot putts to save a par, bogey, or double bogey. We often feel annoyed when these putts don't drop. How realistic are we? To calibrate our expectations, it is useful to examine PGA Tour putting stats. Check out the graph below, which shows average percentages made by U.S. PGA Tour players from various distances over the course of a year.

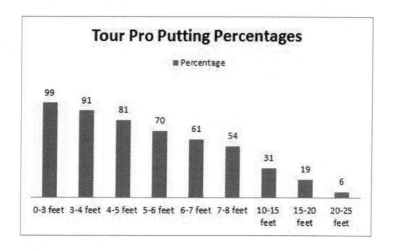

These stats are pretty consistent year after year. This data fascinates me. From distances of three feet to eight feet from the hole, *tour conversion percentages decrease by about ten percent for each additional twelve inches of length.* Assuming the better-than-average weekend golfer will not consistently beat the tour average, we should be thrilled to make a quarter of those eight-to-fifteen-foot "saves" mentioned above. I mention this not to discourage you, but to help set expectations and inform you that even well-struck putts often miss. This awareness is an important element of the BPS because it helps you stay confident in your skill despite missing any given putt. If you convert half your putts from eight feet, you'll be putting like a tour player.

Be Highly Curious About Roll Path

"Reading greens" and predicting roll path are the most challenging and confounding aspects of putting. Yet, they also are the most captivating. If all greens were flat and all putts were dead straight, we would score much better, but the game would soon bore us.

Reading greens is more art than science. The best way to improve your roll path analysis is to develop a healthy *curiosity* about how the ball rolls on the green. Let your curiosity drive your observation. Watch each player's entire roll path with interest on every hole, especially around the cup. There is no need to spin up a lot of verbal mental chatter about what you see. Just soak it all up with your eyes, noticing the surrounding terrain, the subtle slopes near the hole, the speed of the putt, the curve of the path. Simply by observing countless roll paths with curiosity and a relatively quiet mind, you'll gain additional confidence in predicting your own roll paths.

The same curiosity should carry over to your own putts. There are two specific times to exercise your roll path curiosity on each hole. The first is when you are approaching the green. Notice the slopes of the surrounding terrain and the green in general. Find the high points and low points on the green. Wonder how rain water drains off the green. Look around the hole for high and low points. Observe the grain of the grass. Just soak it all in and get a feel for the topographical elements of the entire green.

As you approach each green, identify the high and low areas on the putting surface and the surrounding terrain.

Your curiosity will be replaced briefly by analysis and decision as you consider your specific putt. We'll talk about the elements of your analysis in the next section.

The second time to be curious on each hole is after your putt. After the putter head has moved about five inches past the ball along your selected roll path (and not before!), you look up to observe the line the ball makes on its way to the target. Be careful to watch the ball's entire path until it stops. How well did you predict the roll path? Any surprises? Hmmm. If you learned something and you have time, incorporate the new information and repeat the putt before you leave the green, especially if it was from eight feet or less.

Reading Greens with the GES List

Your intuitive ability to read greens accurately will improve simply by observing, with alert curiosity, lots of putts. In time, you will not need to dissect each factor affecting the roll of the ball; you will simply *feel* where the putt should go. Nevertheless, because many weekend players ask for help in reading greens, I am providing here an overview of the elements which influence the path the ball follows after it leaves the putter head.

When you arrive within fifty yards the green, take a moment or two to notice the surrounding terrain, especially its changes in elevation. Look for the high and low points on the green. Does the whole green slope in a specific direction? Many greens slope back-to-front. Entire greens tend to slope away from mountains and hills and toward bodies of water. Do you see definite tiers or plateaus? These terrain meta-factors can assert domineering influences that create optical illusions and overpower lesser influences around your ball.

For example, if you are playing on a mountainous course, the greens typically will slope down the mountain. You might be facing a putt that clearly appears to curve toward the mountain. You assume the course architect banked the green into the mountainside. When you stroke the putt, however, it surprises you by going dead straight or even sliding away from the mountain. For reasons such as this, it pays handsome dividends to develop the habit of analyzing terrain meta-factors as you approach each green.

Once you are on the green, analyzing your own putt, you can quickly run down a simple checklist I call the *GES List*. GES is an acronym which stands for Grass, Elevation, and Side-slope. My choice of terms is admittedly arbitrary, but hopefully they are easy to remember. Let's consider each in turn.

Grass. Factors to consider about the grass on the green are length, blade thickness, grain, and moisture. When the grass is longer, the green will be slower, and you'll have to hit the putt with more speed to reach the hole. Faster moving putts curve less, so roll paths will be relatively straighter on greens with long grass. On a given green during the summer months, the grass will grow during the day, making putts slower and straighter later in the afternoon. Thicker, coarser blades of grass (i.e., Bermuda blades are longer and thicker than bent grass) also tend to make putts relatively slower and therefore straighter.

However, thicker grasses, such as Bermuda, also tend to have more *grain*, meaning all the blades lie in a similar direction. Grain can exert strong influence on putts: the putt will tend to curve more in the direction the grain lies, and it will roll faster when running down-grain and slower when running into the grain. Grain tends to lie in the direction of the slope; in the direction water runs off the green; with the prevailing wind; and toward the setting sun. You can quickly assess the direction of the grain by observing it from different angles. Grain running away from you (=faster putts) will appear lighter in color and have a silvery sheen, while grain running toward you (=slower putts) will appear relatively darker.

Moisture, on greens, whether from dew, rain, or sprinklers, tends to create more friction, which slows putts and reduces break. If you play in the morning on dew covered greens, you will notice the greens getting faster as the round progresses and the dew dries up. Strong winds tend to dry greens out, making them "sneaky fast." (Of course, the force of strong wind can affect putts, too.)

Elevation. Change in elevation, as I am using it, simply refers to whether the putt is uphill or downhill to the hole. Most players prefer to putt uphill. You can be more aggressive with uphill putts because they decelerate faster than downhill putts; if you hit it past the hole, it will stop sooner. Three putting is less likely. Uphill putts need more speed than downhill putts to go a specific distance to the hole, so they tend to break less overall per given amount of side slope.

However, uphill putts decelerate faster, and they curve more dramatically near the very end of the roll path. They curve less overall than downhill putts, but they do curve more in a short distance near the hole. For this reason, many players tend to miss uphill breaking putts on the low side of the hole and downhill breaking putts on the high side of the hole.

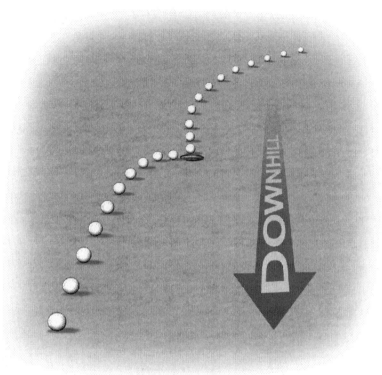

For a given side slope, uphill putts curve less overall, but they break more in a short distance as they lose speed near the hole. Downhill putts curve more overall, but they break comparatively more gradually as they approach the hole.

Some putts are a combination of uphill and downhill. The trickiest of these is the uphill-then-downhill putt. The common tendency is to power the ball up the hill and watch with dismay as it slides far by the hole on the downslope. Three putts are common, as the come-back putt finishes short of the hole. Putts that are downhill-then-uphill are easier overall, but players do tend to see them curve away below the hole.

The best location to determine if your putt is uphill or downhill is from the side of the target line, midway between the ball and the hole, preferably on the low side when there is side-slope. From there you can rotate your head to look first at the ball and then to the hole. It will be easy to see which is higher, even on combination putts. If you have trouble deciding, the elevation change is probably minimal and you can play a level putt.

To see if your putt is uphill or downhill, assess your line from a ninety degree angle on the lower side.

Slope. You scouted the terrain as you approached the green, you examined the grass, and you determined the change in elevation between the ball and the hole. Next, look for changes in side-slope, to the right and left of your target line. Does the area between you and the cup slope right-to-left or left-to-right? If the intervening terrain does not appear to slope in either direction, you have a straight putt. The more severe the side-slope, the more gravity will pull your ball down the slope and the more your roll path will curve.

Look carefully near the hole for changes in side-slope. Does the ground on one side of the hole look higher than the other? Pay particular attention to the side slope in the last third of your roll path, because gravity will have more influence as the putt loses its forward momentum. Likewise, putts with a given side-slope will curve more on faster greens, because the putt has to travel more slowly.

One helpful way to assess side-slope is to search for the *fall line* that runs through the hole. That is, look for the imaginary line on which a ball would roll straight into the hole with no break – basically straight uphill or downhill, depending on whether it starts from a point above or below the hole. Roll paths always curve toward the fall line. When your ball sits to the right of your fall line, your roll path will curve to the left as it approaches the hole. Conversely, when it lies to the left of your fall line, the roll path will curve to the right. This holds true on both downhill and uphill putts. The farther away your ball is from the fall line, the more your roll path is likely to curve on the way to the hole.

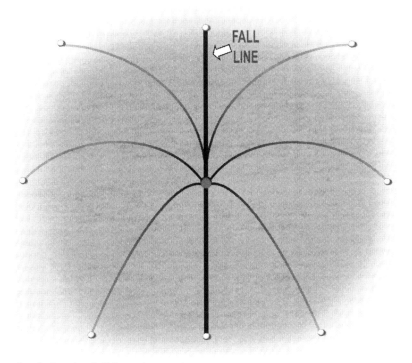

Look for the fall line, from which putts will roll straight uphill or downhill into the hole. Breaking putts curve towards the fall line. The farther away you are from the fall line, the more your putt is likely to break.

Running through your GES List can take fifteen to thirty seconds, depending on the complexities of each factor. Typically, analysis of grass and elevation is relatively quick, while analysis of side-slope takes a bit longer, especially if you look for the fall line.

I must emphasize that this GES work is *perceptual*. Merely obscrve the specific elements of grass, elevation, and side-slope and trust your subconscious mind to perform the calculations needed to predict roll path. It is a miracle of the human mind that you can simply observe all the GES factors without a lot of verbal mental chatter, and your imagination will create images of how your ball is likely to roll over the terrain.

Now that we have a quick overview of GES factors influencing roll path, we can focus on how to select our ideal roll path from among the many possibilities.

Exercise Your Imagination

Although I tried to keep the GES List simple, it is easy to see that analyzing factors that affect roll path can drive you goofy, especially on fast, sloping greens. The antidote, as mentioned earlier, is simple curiosity. Simply add your observations to your mental computer and engage your imagination. You might even say aloud to yourself, "How is this putt going to roll into the hole?"

Most instructors will stress the importance of visualization in picking a roll path, and I agree. However, many students lament that they have trouble visualizing, so let us simply enlist our *imaginations*. Everyone can imagine a golf ball rolling along a green into the hole to some extent, and it gets easier with practice.

After completing your GES List observations (grass/elevation/slope), position yourself in a crouching position behind the ball on the line to the cup. Position your eyes as low as possible and parallel to the ground to engage your binocular vision effectively. Imagine the ball rolling along a path and falling into the hole. (We will talk about the speed at which the ball enters the cup in subsequent lessons. It changes for different types of putts.

For now, imagine enough speed to hit the back of the cup half way down.)

Crouch low a few paces behind your ball and actively imagine your ideal roll path and your ball dropping into the hole.

You might entertain several different paths until one feels better than the others. Be as specific as possible. *Imagine the circumference of the hole as the face of a clock* and imagine which number the ball will roll over – often somewhere between five and seven o'clock. Then imagine the entire roll path again, seeing if you can pick out any intermediate targets – small discolorations in the green – on the way to the hole. Some teachers recommend finding an intermediate target on the roll path within a foot or so of the ball. This is great if you can find one, as it will facilitate aiming the putter head during your preshot routine. If you do not see one, do not worry about it.

Imagine the circumference of the hole as the face of a clock and decide which number the ball will roll over to enter the cup.

If your imagination needs a catalyst, talking to yourself might do the trick. Whisper quietly, "I see it running at a good clip to the brown spot about two feet from the hole, then curving slightly left into the cup at five o'clock." Verbalizing a desired image invariably stimulates the imagination to produce it. Do not be shy about this!

One common challenge is seeing several feasible lines the ball could take to the hole. You imagine one possible line, than another slightly different one, then another one, and so on. This can get completely out of control, especially on putts with a lot of side-hill break. My first recommendation is to avoid imaging *lines*, and instead try to envision a *path* about four inches wide that leads into the cup. I like to imagine painting a white or yellow path with a four inch paint roller. Simply roll it onto the green in your imagination. I do this, and it always reduces the number of lines I see.

Another effective way to reduce the number of lines your imagination conjures is to envision precisely where the ball enters the cup *and the speed at which it hits the back of the cup*. Give your mental computer a precise picture of ball speed and it will respond with a specific roll path.

Select a prospective roll path that elicits an affirmative nod of your head. Keep it fresh and alive in your imagination.

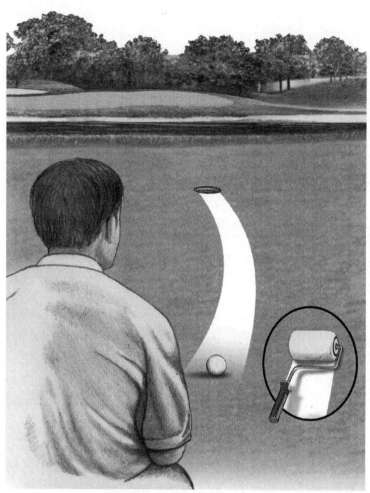

To reduce the number of possible roll paths you see on breaking putts, imagine your ball rolling along a four-inch wide roll path.

The next step is to rehearse the *feeling* of the stroke required to produce the roll path by taking a practice swing from the same spot a couple of feet behind the ball. In essence, you expand your imagining process to include the *anticipated kinesthetic feeling* of the appropriate stroke force. This is the same process you use before you shoot a basketball at the hoop, throw a pitch, or toss a soda can into a trash bin.

Stand up from your crouching position, facing the hole. Continue to use your binocular vision to imagine the ball moving along the roll path at an appropriate speed. Now take a practice swing or two, actively *feeling* the motion that will propel the ball at your imagined speed. This might sound complicated, but it is a process your eyes, mind, and body do all the time in one form or another.

Chances are, after you make the first practice stroke, your body will automatically assess how accurate it was and will generate a second stroke at a calibrated speed. Of course, the more you practice this, the more comfortable and useful it becomes. For any given putt, one to three practice strokes should suffice from down the target line. You usually can accomplish this in between the putts of other players in your group; you don't have to wait until it's your turn to putt.

The Unconflicted Mind

You were curious about roll path, you analyzed the green with GES, and you unleased your imagination to visualize the path your putt will traverse to the hole, and you anticipated the feeling of the putt during one or more practice strokes. The next crucial element in preparation for the bulletproof stroke is achieving the state of **unconflicted mind**. In other words, your analysis and imagining are followed by *mental and emotional* *commitment.* You commit to a roll path and embrace it, not with trepidation, but with robust enthusiasm. Your mind and heart say, "Yes, that's it!" You move forward into your set up and stroke with absolute conviction regarding what you are about to do. Errant, disruptive, negative thoughts simply *ARE NOT ALLOWED*. If necessary, you talk (or whisper) to yourself, describing again how the ball will roll along your desired path.

Maybe you have picked an excellent roll path, maybe not; *it does not matter.* All that does matter at this juncture is your complete, coherent commitment to your roll path, including any intermediate target(s) you have selected. You arise from your crouch to approach the ball, with a vivid vision of the roll path and absolute certainty that you soon will stroke the ball along that vivid path, into the hole.

The unconflicted mind is vital for two reasons. First, it overcomes the natural tendency to second guess your selected roll path after you assume your putting stance. In your stance, your eyes view the terrain from the ball to the hole from a much different angle than you had when crouching to view the line from behind the ball. This "new information" often causes uncertainty and doubt about the roll path you selected moments before. It is important to understand and believe that your down-line crouch position gives you better information because your eyes are parallel to the ground and looking directly up the target line. You must trust the initial line and ignore any new perspective you get when standing over your putt. As we will discuss in Lesson 3, there is no room or time during your in-stroke routine for doubts and second guesses.

The second great value of the unconflicted mind is the confidence it gives to your putting stroke. Because you are certain you selected a good roll path, you have the patience to allow the bulletproof putting stroke to place the ball on that path, *all in good time*. You enjoy the feeling of coherent confidence, so you do not rush your stroke because of fear, uncertainty, or doubt. You simply allow yourself to produce the flawless pace and rhythm of your bulletproof stroke.

Quick Review

Anticipating and predicting ideal roll path at appropriate ball speeds is the great challenge of putting. Subtle nuances of putting surface and surrounding terrain complicate the task and force us to pay close attention on even the most trivial of putts. To improve your chances of success at reading greens and selecting roll paths, I offered four recommendations.

Be realistic about your chances. The world's best golfers sink about half their eight foot putts, and they miss about one-third of their six-footers. Needless to say, they practice a lot more than the typical weekend player. Bearing this in mind will reduce the natural tendency to get down on yourself after a couple of missed putts.

Stay highly curious about roll path and reading greens. Reading greens is the study of a lifetime. The more interest and attention you place on watching balls roll on the green – yours and everyone else's – the faster you will gain confidence in your ability to read greens accurately. After examining the surrounding terrain on every hole, employ the GES List to estimate the likely effects of grass, elevation, and side-slope.

Exercise your imagination. Most of the work in putting is done with the mind. Once your GES analysis is loaded into your mental computer, enthusiastically engage your imagination to *see* the best ball speed and roll path and *feel* the stroke that will create it.

Be decisive. If you trust your analysis and imagination, you are ready to engage your emotions and approach your putt with an unconflicted mind – with absolute confidence and certainty about your chosen roll path and your ability to roll your putt along it.

In Lesson 3, we blend your green reading abilities with your repeatable stroke in a bulletproof ***shot routine***. In Lesson 4, we develop strategies and techniques for four types of putts, modifying your bulletproof routine ever-so-slightly for slam dunk, drillable, drainable, and lag putts.

Lesson 3 –Your Bulletproof Routine

"You should establish both a routine and a ritual for every putt you face."
-Dave Pelz, *Dave Pelz's Putting Bible*

"All good putters have a consistent routine...With the best putters the movements preceding and during the stroke are identical, and the time elapsed from the moment they take their stance to the moment of impact doesn't vary."
-Ray Floyd, *The Elements of Scoring*

"Regardless of your routine – and there are lots of variations – the key is to perform it exactly the same way on every putt."
-Tiger Woods, *How I Play Golf*

This lesson is short but extremely important. If you ignore all the advice in the rest of this book, yet embrace the concept of routine, your putting will improve. The typical weekend golfer does not bother with a putting routine, so I included the three quotes above to highlight the great value – yea, the *necessity* – of developing and using a consistent putting routine. The pros do it and you should, too.

Even though great putting involves abstract, right-brain concepts such as imagination, feel, and confidence, your *thoughts and actions* before and during the putting stroke must be controlled with military precision. This precision is embodied in a specific series of steps, a *routine*, which you execute in the same manner and sequence on every putt.

Why bother with the restrictive constraints of a routine? Why not just flow freely and let every putt be a unique, creative act? Two reasons. First, a habitual routine ensures you perform all the vital steps of analyzing, imagining, assuming your stance, and stroking the putt in the ideal order. Second and most importantly, your routine completely monopolizes your conscious attention, leaving no room for invasion by negative and fearful thoughts. In essence, your routine helps you execute your stroke with an unconflicted mind.

You might be tempted to dispense with routine and simply intend to stand over each put until you are confident in the outcome. But what happens if the confidence never comes, and FUD intervenes instead? The longer you stand over the putt feeling uncertain, the more likely you are to become anxious and self-conscious and to make a lousy stroke. With a good routine, you simply go about your business and wait for the putt to drop.

Your routine is not mere busy-work; every element is essential. Initially, working through the steps in precise order is a chore, and your putting probably will suffer for a few days; but you must stick with it. Soon enough, your routine becomes habitual, and the benefits are yours to keep. You might be tempted from time to time to break from your routine and take longer than usual over a putt, analyzing the subtleties of a roll path or fiddling with your alignment. I strongly encourage you to overcome this temptation. Stick with your routine; learn to trust it and depend on it.

You should and shall develop your own, personalized routine. I will offer suggestions but the final choice is yours. Watch other players on TV or at your club and mimic those elements that appeal to you. Experiment a bit, but do not fiddle endlessly. Decide on your routine and commit to it. Modify your routine only after careful deliberation. I suggest writing down your routine on an index card and referring to it on the golf course until it becomes habitual. After some initial discomfort, you'll probably learn to enjoy your routine.

There are three general parts to your routine: 1) predicting the roll path and speed, 2) assuming your stance, and 3) stroking your putt. Let us discuss each in turn.

Predicting Roll Path and Speed

As we covered in detail in the last lesson, there is a process for deciding where to aim your putter. It involves analyzing the factors likely to influence your roll path and then engaging your imagination to predict how the ball should roll into the hole. Fortunately, much of this process can be accomplished while waiting for others to chip or putt. Because we covered many of these steps in Lesson 2, I will summarize them here in bullet format.

- Observe the surrounding terrain as you walk up to the green. Consider nearby hills and water bodies. Find the high and low spots on the green. Imagine how water drains off the green.

You must develop a consistent routine for each element of the putt: 1) predicting the roll path and speed, 2) assuming your stance, and 3) stroking your putt.

- Mark your ball and fix your ball mark. Clean your ball. (Never putt with a dirty ball.)
- Start your GES List analysis by inspecting the grass and the grain.
- If the flow of play permits, position yourself briefly ninety degrees to the line of your putt, on the downslope side, about halfway between your ball and the hole. Check the change in elevation. Is your putt uphill or downhill?
- Position yourself behind your ball, downline from the hole. Crouch low and study the prospective roll path to analyze side slope. Pay special attention to

slope changes near the hole, where the roll path will be most affected.

- Imagine the roll path the ball will follow into the hole. Experiment with different possibilities until one roll path intuitively feels right. *Imagine, as vividly as you can, the path and the speed the ball will roll along it.* If the putt is a breaking putt, look for intermediate targets along the path to help you aim. In essence, your "roll path and speed" decision is made, doubts or other possibilities are excluded, and positive images are filling your mind repetitively.

- When it is your turn to putt, replace your ball, pick up your marker, and return briefly to your crouching position. Imagine your role path and pick an intermediate target at which to aim (more on this in the next lesson).

- Stand up, still a few pace or two behind the ball, facing the target, and continue imagining your roll path. While gazing at the roll path and target, take one or two practice strokes, *feeling* the ideal stroke to roll the ball at the desired speed. *The primary goal is to let your unconflicted imagination create a kinesthetic rehearsal of the proper stroke.*

- At this moment, a feeling of confidence and positive expectancy should motivate you to approach the putt.

Assuming Your Stance

We covered the ideal stance for the bullet proof stroke in Lesson 1, so let us incorporate it into your routine through a few simple steps.

- As you walk to stand astride your ball, keep your eyes on the target at which you will aim your putter. This could be a spot on the circumference of the hole or an intermediate target along the roll path, as we will discuss in the next lesson.
- Your putter should be in your target-side (typically left) hand, in the proper grip position.
- As you approach the ball, still looking at the target, place your right foot in position, along a line parallel to the target line.
- Position the putter behind the ball, facing the target, and place your other hand on the grip. Place your left foot on the same line as the right foot, parallel to your target line.
- Assume your putting stance, with your eyes directly over the target line and your hands directly under your shoulders, which also are parallel to your target line.
- You now take two "looks." The first look aims your putter at your target, so you look first at your putter's aiming guide, following its line to your target. (You do this by rotating your head only; do not let your shoulders or spine change position.)

Look again at your aiming guide and adjust if necessary.

- On your second look, verify that your putter's aiming guide is aligned to your target, and - as you look at the target - imagine the ball rolling over your target and into the cup at an appropriate speed, and hitting the back of the cup at the appropriate spot.

Stroking Your Putt

I had a good deal to say about the bulletproof stroke in Lesson 1, and I encourage you to review it now. Hopefully, after you initially finished Lesson 1, you practiced your stroke until you gained solid confidence in your ability to swing the putter along a straight line for five inches on each side of the ball.

At this point in the putting process, all the work is finished and you allow your body to make the stroke without any interference from FUD. This part of your routine takes only a couple of seconds. You completed your two "looks," and you have a fresh image of the ball rolling to the target and hitting the back of the cup at the desired speed. Stroke the putt before anxious feelings impinge on you, before fear of missing the putt ruins the timing and rhythm of your stroke.

- As you finish your final look at the target and return your gaze to the ball, your conscious attention should *associate/connect the ball with the target* and allow your body to make your bulletproof pendulum stroke along the target line at a length and a pace that *feels* right.

- The emphasis is on *feel*. The analysis is complete; the imagining is complete. Now *feeling* takes over. In essence, you *anticipate the feeling* of the appropriate stroke and then observe yourself as you execute it. I particularly like the image discussed earlier of a rubber band attached to the target and the putter shaft. I feel as if I am stretching the rubber band on the back stroke and letting the rubber band pull the putter to the target on the forward stroke.

- Patience is paramount. The conscious mind waits patiently, in a state of positive expectancy, for the putting stroke to occur. A mental state of detached observation is surprisingly effective. You simply gaze at the ball and *wait* while your stroke rolls the ball along the imagined path. Brad Faxon, one of the game's best putters, put it this way, "Believe it or not, I'm not really thinking about anything when I putt. I let my instincts take over."

Many makeable putts are missed because the weekend player tries too hard to steer the putt and force the ball into the hole. Often, the hands get active and twist the clubface off line. The tempo is rushed and rhythm is ruined when the downswing starts too soon and too fast. The ball can either rocket past the target, or it can come up short if the stroke decelerates into the ball.

While the ideal mental state during the stroke is a combination of *positive expectancy* and *detached observation*, sometimes it is nearly impossible to keep intent, or will-power, from asserting itself. Because the putt seems so important, the mind simply must try to DO something. (This urge is especially urgent when you lack trust in your stroke.) If you feel you must *try to control* some aspect of the stroke, there are two workable options to include in this part of your routine.

The first option is to focus on rhythm. Recall your ideal rhythm and place your intent during the stroke on creating that rhythm. For me, this involves a brief pause at the end of the backswing and a slow start to the forward stroke.

The second option for asserting control during the stroke is to focus on the follow-through, and endeavor to keep the putter shaft and head (and/or your hands) moving along the target line at a comfortable pace for four or more inches through the ball position. This simple act of making the putter follow the ball toward the target can help you sink putts despite the vexing presence of FUD.

Whether you need to *do* something, or you can simply wait while your body strokes the putt, the key aspect of this section of your routine is to stroke the putt and roll the ball *as soon as your two "looks" are completed*. This has to occur while the image of the ball rolling to the target is still fresh in your mind. The longer you stand over the ball, checking and rechecking your aim, the more likely you are to start fidgeting and feeling anxious.

I do realize it has been said by some great putters, notably Jack Nicklaus, that you should not stroke the putt until you believe you can make it. Who can argue with that sentiment? The Golden Bear was one of the greatest clutch putters in history, and he often stood for long moments over a putt before knocking it into the hole under immense tournament pressure. For the weekend golfer, though, this is a recipe for disaster. For most of us, the longer we stand over a putt, the more likely we are to get attacked by FUD.

If you do an enthusiastic job of imagining the roll path and speed, and you keep the image fresh in your mind as you assume your stance, I predict you will putt better by taking two "looks" (three at the most) and immediately stroking your putt with patience. You may never achieve the absolute conviction that you will make each putt, but you surely can achieve a state of positive expectancy and of confidence in your stroke.

Making Your Routine Automatic

The sooner your routine becomes habitual, the sooner you will experience the pleasures of bulletproof putting. What is the fastest way to get there? Start by breaking your training into two phases: pre-shot and in-shot. Pre-shot entails your roll path analysis, and it is learned best on actual putting greens. In-shot includes your set up and stroke and it can be memorized easily at home.

I recommend focusing first on your in-shot routine. Ideally, you should procure a practice putting rug similar to the *SKLZ Accelerator*. I like this mat because it has alignment/stroke guides and it encourages you to putt firmly on short putts.

That said, you can do nearly as well by putting on a carpet, using a coin as a target. Commit to spending five minutes a day, every day, for a month to ingrain your set up and stroke routine. Don't worry about making putts for the first couple of weeks. Simply repeat with military precision the exact steps in your in-shot routine. Yes, we want this to become as habitual and automatic as shaving with a razor.

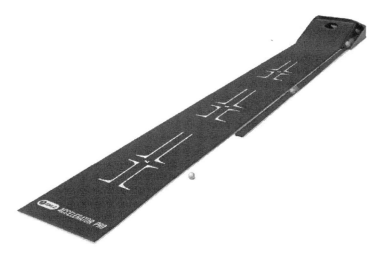

Master your in-shot routine by practicing a few minutes each day on an indoor carpet or putting matt, such as the SKLZ Accelerator.

Pay particular attention to *what you are thinking* immediately before and during the actual stroke. We want it to be *the same every time*. We do not want your mind wandering into FUD territory! If you prefer to speak each step mentally to yourself initially, that is fine. After a couple of weeks, your routine will become automatic and you won't have to recite the steps to yourself.

As you gaze at the ball and stroke your putt, you might occupy your mind by reciting a short phrase, such as "one-and-two," or "teeter...totter," or "sole to sole, in the hole." Talking to yourself can occupy your mind while your body makes its ingrained stroke.

When you have repeated your in-shot routine diligently and frequently enough to make it feel natural and automatic, you'll be ready to expand your routine to include the pre-shot activities. This involves reading breaks on real greens. You'll need to set aside a handful of fifteen to twenty minute sessions on a practice green, because trying to institute a new routine during an actual round of golf is sure to prove catastrophic. Initially, don't even bother to hit putts. Just throw a handful of balls around the putting green and practice going through the pre-shot steps in exactly the same manner every time. If it helps, write your steps on an index card and refer to it until your process becomes automatic.

Once your pre-shot routine is ingrained, you can add the set-up and stroke routine you learned at home. The whole process soon should feel comfortable and automatic.

Quick Review of Routine

A consistent routine is *mandatory* for bulletproof putting, primarily because it provides your essential defense against anxiety and FUD. There are three general parts to your routine: 1) predicting the roll path and speed, 2) assuming your stance, and 3) stroking your putt. In part one, you exercise your imagination and sense of kinesthetic anticipation. In part two, you keep these sensations alive while you align your body and aim your putter. In part three, you let *feel* take over and you stroke the putt while your conscious mind gazes at the ball and waits with patience and positive expectancy.

The exact details of your routine should be unique to you. Work it out over time on the practice green or at home. Do not be surprised or concerned if you putt worse in the beginning because learning a new habit is taxing and distracting. Stick with it, however, and your putting will improve measurably in a remarkably short time.

In the next lesson, we will discuss techniques and strategies for four types of putts: slam dunks, drillable, drainable, and lag putts. I will suggest very minor modifications to your routine to deal with the subtle differences among these putts. For the most part, though, the routine you developed in this lesson will be valuable on every putt you face.

Lesson 4 - Conquering the Four Types of Putts

"The most important shot in golf is the six foot putt."
-Ray Floyd, *The Elements of Scoring*

"In putting you are confronted by two truths difficult to reconcile. If you don't get the ball up, it can't go in. But for each added bit of speed it has less of the hole to hit."
-Paul Runyan, *The Short Way to Lower Scoring*

Introducing the Four Types of Putts

If you have been thoughtful in your reading and practice thus far, you probably are feeling optimistic and increasingly confident in your ability to read greens accurately and to make a consistent putting stroke. Developing a precise, habitual routine takes a bit longer, and I hope you are working on that with genuine commitment. In this lesson, we'll refine your strategy and modify your routine just a bit to master four different types of putts. We will discuss each in turn.

- **Slam dunks** – very short putts you rarely miss
- **Drillable** – makeable putts you can drill straight into the cup
- **Drainable** – makeable putts that require you to aim outside the cup to allow for break
- **Lag** – longer, lower-percentage putts that you intend to leave close enough to set up a slam dunk.

You might wonder why a supposedly streamlined system for the weekend golfer forces you to master four different kinds of putts. Am I complicating things needlessly? Given that putting comprises at least forty percent of your strokes and the other sixty percent requires a formidable variety of shotmaking skills, it seems reasonable to categorize each putt you face into one of only four categories. The differences in approach to each type are subtle and easily learned. As you will see, modifying your mind-set and routine slightly to handle different types of putts will yield significant benefits.

Slam Dunks

These putts, by definition, are whatever length you can expect to sink at least ninety-five percent of the time. For PGA Tour players, these are putts of three feet or less, but for the rest of us, they are probably two feet or less. Although far from the most exciting shots in golf, they count the same on the scorecard as 300-yard drives. Missing one is like taking a penalty shot at the conclusion of the hole.

Most players call these tap-ins or gimmies, and they often don't give these putts the respect they deserve. They abandon all elements of their routine and simply step up and slap the ball. Perhaps they feel silly going through their whole routines for such short putts. If they miss one, they tell themselves it was a gimmie and they could have made it if they had tried. This probably is true, of course, but a little seed of FUD germinates every time this happens.

I call these putts *slam dunks*, rather than tap-ins, because they are the ultimate, close-in scoring shots, and they should be struck with focus and confidence. While there is no need to run through your entire putting routine for each slam dunk, it does make sense to execute the same mini-routine on every slam dunk. The primary goal is simple: roll the ball straight into the center of the hole with enough speed to strike the back of the cup about one inch below the surface. This amount of speed, or pace, will keep the ball on line despite any change in slope or imperfections on the putting surface. Because you are hitting a short, straight putt, you usually can forego your GES analysis, but you still must imagine your roll path, take your stance, and make a solid stroke.

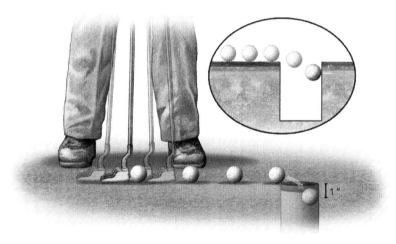

Slam dunk putts carry enough speed to strike the back of the cup about one inch below the surface.

Here's an example of a sensible mini-routine for slam dunks:

1. Maintain the sense of deliberateness and focus you bring to every putt.
2. Imagine/visualize the ball rolling straight into the center of the cup at the appropriate speed to strike the back of the cup one inch below the surface.
3. Take your normal putting stance, aligned parallel to the target line. This is important because is it a requisite precursor to a repeatable stroke.
4. Make your bulletproof putting stroke with good rhythm, ensuring that your hands and putter follow-through to the target.

Remember to treat each slam dunk as an opportunity to execute your disciplined mini-routine, and you'll avoid those embarrassing woulda-coulda-shoulda moments on the putting greens.

By the way, if you *ever* feel uncertain or doubtful over a so-called slam dunk putt, please mark the ball, step back, and go through your drillable putt routine, as described in the next section.

Drillable Putts

The *drillable putt* may be the most important shot in golf. Become skilled at drillable putts, and your game will reach a higher level. Your scores will drop and your confidence will soar.

A drillable putt is *one you can sink by aiming your putter at a point along the front circumference of the cup and drilling the putt straight into the hole.* As you look at the cup downline from your ball position, pretend the cup's circumference is the outline of a clock. The point closest to you on the front circumference can be viewed as six o'clock, and the right and left edges are three and nine o'clock, respectively.

Drillable putts are those you can comfortably aim at a spot between five and seven o'clock on the face, believing a firmly struck putt will roll over the six o'clock point. In other words, the putt will break only about an inch or less on its way to the front of the cup. The green's slope and speed are mellow enough to let you to hit your putt with sufficient pace to keep it straight, without the risk of knocking it too far past the hole if you miss.

How long are drillable putts? Of course, the answer always depends on your GES analysis about the speed and slope of the green and the degree of break in your putt. If the green is super-fast and sloped, you won't find many drillable putts over a few feet in length. In general, though, they range from two to six or seven feet in length. Occasionally, they can be much longer – typically on flat, slow greens – and the principles presented here still apply.

As we know, faster rolling putts tend to break less than slower rolling putts, hence the term *drillable*. You *drill* these putts into the cup, and they strike the back of the hole about two inches below the surface. Ideally, you hit them with enough speed to minimize break and to overcome minor disruptions in the putting surface, while leaving them within slam dunk range if you miss.

Let me strongly emphasize the need to imagine or visualize the ball rolling over the desired spot on the front of the cup *with sufficient speed to strike the back of the cup* about two inches from the top. If you neglect to imagine the ball hitting the back of the cup, you might decelerate on the stroke and fail to strike the ball with enough speed to stay on line as it rolls over surface imperfections near the cup.

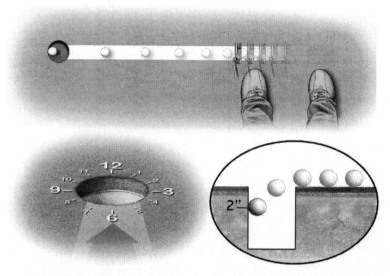

Stroke your drillable putts at a spot within the center two inches of the cup, with enough force to strike the back of the cup about two inches below the surface.

The critical element of success with drillable putts is the unshakable belief that you have trained yourself to 1) aim correctly and 2) stroke the putter along a straight line for a few inches on each side of the ball. If you can do these two things reliably, you can hit a straight putt with astounding consistency. With this confidence, you will drill straight putts into the hole with impressive aplomb and refreshing regularity.

To help you aim correctly on drillable putts, I'll repeat a piece of advice I offered in the Lesson 1: use a golf ball alignment marker to draw a stripe on the circumference of your ball. From behind the ball, as part of your pre-shot routine, point the stripe at your target (a spot between 5 and 7 o'clock on the front of the cup). This takes practice. At first, you might have trouble aligning to the target, but you must keep at it until you feel comfortable and confident with this important element of your pre-shot routine. It is worth the investment of time to practice aligning the stripe at a target for a couple of minutes a day at home or in the office. If you get frustrated and are tempted to abandon this tactic, I urge you to reconsider. Many of the best players in the world use this technique, and you should, too.

After you position your stripe, synchronize the alignment guide on your putter with the stripe on your ball, and set up with your body parallel to that target line. Trust the stripe! (In the stance, right handers might feel as if the stripe is misaligned to the left.) As you make your stroke, you should see the stripe roll consistently along the target line, straight into the cup. It is a good feeling, so stick with it.

(Although I strongly recommend using the stripe for *drillable* putts, which essentially are straight putts, I consider the stripe optional for both drainable and lag putts, for reasons I'll explain later in this lesson.)

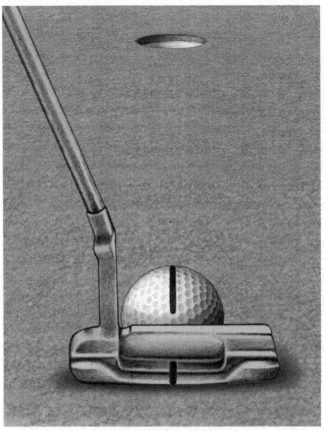

You will sink more drillable putts by aiming the stripe on your ball at a spot on or close to the center of the cup's front edge.

Here's a summary description of how you slightly modify your routine for drillable putts:

1. Maintain the sense of deliberateness and focus you bring to every putt.
2. When you determine in your pre shot routine that the putt is pretty straight and you can aim at a spot between 5 and 7 o'clock on the rim of the hole, say

to yourself, with confidence, "This is a drillable putt!"

3. Before you pick up your ball marker, position yourself behind the ball, down the target line from the hole, and aim the stripe at the spot on the rim of the cup, between 5 and 7 o'clock.

4. If necessary (especially when you first start using the stripe), take a few steps back down the target line and check that the stripe is aimed appropriately. If it needs a little nudge, do so. Don't worry; you'll get skilled with practice. Then pick up your ball marker.

5. Take your normal putting stance, first aligning the guide on your putter head to the stripe on the ball and then aligning your body parallel to the stripe.

6. Imagine/visualize the ball rolling into the center of the cup at the appropriate speed to hit into the back of the cup about two inches from the top.

7. Watch the stripe on the top of the ball as you make your bulletproof putting stroke with good rhythm, ensuring that you follow-through straight to the target.

8. Watch the stripe roll end over end into the hole.

Drainable Putts

The *drainable putt* may be the most confounding, frustrating shot in golf. Yet, it can also be the most rewarding putt to sink. It is the breaking putt from fifteen feet or less that you feel you *should* make, but often miss by the slimmest of margins when it curves too much or too little to drop into the hole.

Potentially *drillable* putts become *drainable* instead when you realize two things during your preshot analysis. First, you sense that, to keep the putt straight enough to be drillable, you'll have to hit it so hard that a missed putt will roll well outside slam dunk range. Second, you see that (at a reasonable speed) your roll path will curve so much that you cannot aim for a spot between five and seven o'clock on the front of the cup. In other words, *the ball is going to curve more than a couple of inches when rolled at an acceptable speed*. In most cases, the ball needs to enter the hole from two o'clock to five o'clock on the right, or from seven o'clock to ten o'clock on the left. Your target for aligning your putter will be near or outside the right or left perimeters of the cup.

So, what's the big deal? Why are these putts so confounding? How are they so different from slam dunks and drillable putts? The simple answer is – in contrast to slam dunks and drillable putts – there is no single, correct roll path for any given drainable putt. Depending on how hard the putt is struck, the ball can take many different curving paths to the hole. If, for example, your caddie says to aim two inches outside the hole, the unknown, unspoken factor is *at what speed of putt*? If you do start the ball on the correct line, but your speed is a tad too fast or too slow, you'll miss the putt high or low. In short, the drainable putt must be hit on the appropriate line *for the speed at which it starts rolling*. Clearly – to me, at least – the reason tour players only sink about half their putts from seven to eight feet is that a large percentage of those putts curve too much to be drillable.

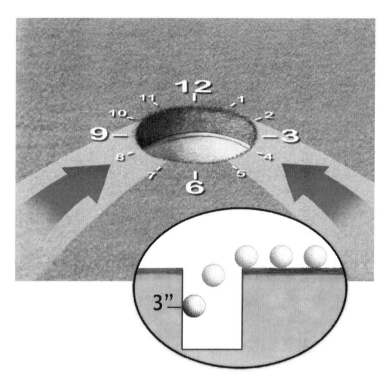

Your drainable putts frequently will enter the hole between two and five o'clock or seven and ten o'clock, and most should strike the back of the cup about halfway down.

I call these curving putts *drainable* because they (along with lag putts) involve a completely different mindset from drillable and slam dunk putts, and the term drainable conjures an image of the putt being sucked down the drain like water swirls down a sink. Drainable putts require more finesse and a higher degree of *feel*. Recall that with slam dunk and drillable putts, our bulletproof putting mechanics overpower gravity and slope and knock the ball smartly into the cup. For drainable putts, we flow with the slope and surrender to gravity; we start the ball rolling and let nature take its course, so to speak. In our parlance, drillable equals dominance, and drainable equals collaboration with slope and gravity.

When you set up to the drainable putt, the tricky issue always is...*where to aim*. This is a primary difference between drainable putts and drillable and slam dunks, where the putter is aimed more or less directly at the ball's entry spot on the cup. On drainable putts, we aim the putter face somewhere "outside" the entry spot on the cup, to account for the curve of the roll path. Picking this intermediate target is tricky, as there are various, speed-dependent possibilities.

Determining the ideal roll path on drainable putts requires us to imagine - at the same time - the speed of the ball along the path. Because putts break more as they slow down, we endeavor to keep as much speed as possible on the ball without rolling outside slam dunk range if we miss. *Staying within slam dunk range is vitally important because we are likely to miss a significant percentage of drainable putts, and we do not want to three-putt.* So, we visualize the ball rolling into the cup with enough speed to hit the back of the cup about three inches below the surface, depending on the slope and speed of the green. (The only time you want to imagine a drainable putt barely having enough speed to die into the front of the hole is when you are facing a very fast, downhill putt.)

Since we have to decide upon both a line and a speed, which should we pick first? The answer is both simultaneously, actually. I recommend first imagining the ball rolling the last twelve inches or so up to the hole and crossing a specific spot on the rim of the cup (ex., four o'clock) at the appropriate speed (typically to hit the back of the cup about half-way down). Once we clearly see that image a couple of times, we then start at the ball and visualize the entire roll path, ending with the climactic scene we already imagined. It can be helpful to identify a couple of intermediate spots along the roll path, such as discolorations and old ball marks, but we don't want to focus so intently on these as targets that we lose the feel of ball speed along the roll path.

The primary information we want to instill in our minds and bodies on drainable putts is *visualization of the ball crossing the correct spot on the circumference of the cup at a reasonable speed*. We then trust our bodies to select the appropriate path along which to roll the ball to reach our desired entry point, as well as the appropriate stroke to produce the imagined ball speed.

The combination of visualization-of-path and preview-of-stroke is paramount on drainable putts. We let our bodies rehearse and experience the anticipated kinesthetic feeling of the stroke that combines the ideal roll path and speed. This mental-rehearsal process is similar to how we use our bodies to throw an object such as a ball or Frisbee to a target.

I realize I still have not answered the not-so-simple question of where to aim the putter when you set up to a drainable putt. Sure, you imagine the ball rolling the final twelve inches and over the edge of the cup at a good speed, but where do you aim the putter?

One temptation – and a common misconception – is to pick a spot on the roll path a bit short of the hole, and think of it as the apex of the putt. We tend to think to ourselves, "I'll hit it straight at that spot, and it will curve into the hole from there." Unfortunately, as Dave Pelz and others famously demonstrate, the apex of the putt typically occurs *at the ball position*, meaning gravity pulls the ball downhill as soon as it leaves the clubface. When you aim and stroke the putt straight at your intermediate target, you are likely to miss that target, and probably the hole, on the downhill side. If you use this aiming technique, observe your results carefully to look for this tendency to miss low. An easy cure is to keep the ball on the uphill side of your typical intermediate target.

Another useful and time-tested technique on drainable putts is to pick a spot hole-high on either side of the cup and aim at that, letting gravity pull the ball toward the hole from that line. This can work well, provided that you use the spot to aim the putter and then, before you start the stroke, refocus your imagination on the ball rolling into the cup. If, instead, you keep looking at that alignment target all through your preshot routine, you might subconsciously adjust your stroke and mistakenly roll the ball over that spot outside the cup.

Weekend golfers suffer from this tendency, so be aware of whether it happens to you. You'll know it is, if you often miss your putts on the high side of the cup. You might say, "I missed it on the pro side," or "I hit it through the break," but be aware that you may be simply rolling the ball over your alignment target.

You overcome this tendency, again, by "soft aiming" the putter at that spot outside the point of entry, and then refocusing your attention on the *point of entry and the anticipated feeling of the stroke* along your aim-line that gives you the appropriate ball speed to achieve your entry point. You anticipate the feeling of setting the ball on its roll path and letting it follow the pull of gravity down the drain, into the cup. It can be helpful, as you prepare to stroke the putt, to imagine a powerful suction force emanating from the cup that pulls in everything that comes anywhere close, like a black hole in outer space.

I want to emphasize the profound differences between drillable and drainable putts. For a drillable putt, we aim our stripe on the ball and the alignment guide on the putter directly at the chosen entry point along the front of the circumference of the cup. Then we stroke the putter strictly along that line and drill the ball directly into the back of the cup. The process is mechanistic, the mindset is resolute. In stark contrast, the drainable putt requires a sense of touch and finesse. Although we still actively visualize the ball rolling over the appropriate entry spot on the cup, we don't (necessarily) use the stripe on the ball, and our putter alignment may be a bit fuzzy, even indistinct. We trust our bodies, at the moment of the stroke, to select the precise combination of roll path and speed to achieve the entry point. Our minds simply wait while our bodies *feel* the putt into the hole.

Because these two approaches are so different, it is essential to determine whether a given putt is drillable or drainable. In my opinion, drainable putts are more fun but drillable putts are easier; so the first choice should always be drillable. As you assess your putt, ask yourself how it feels to imagine drilling the ball straight into the hole. If it feels good, say to yourself, with conviction, "This putt is *drillable!*"

If the idea of drilling feels uncomfortable, you probably surmise that you'd have to smack it too hard to keep it on a straight line, and a missed attempt would blow well outside your slam dunk range. Fine, you'll have to aim the putter somewhere outside the entry point and stroke the putt with more finesse, and the ball will curve into the side of the hole. Say to yourself, "This putt is *drainable...*" Adjust your thinking accordingly and call forth a heightened sense of feel and finesse.

What about the grey zone, those nerve-wracking putts on the margin between drillable and drainable? Should you drill them or drain them? Consider, for example, a fairly level six foot putt that slopes left to right. You sense you could drill it, but you'd have to aim at or just outside the left edge. Should you drill it? My suggestion is this: drill only those putts that can be aimed *inside the cup* with outer boundaries of four and eight o'clock. As a general rule, I do not recommend drilling putts at or just outside the edge of the hole, because of the tendency to blow the putt straight over the edge of the cup or spin it out. With drilled putts, the ball is travelling faster and is less likely to catch an edge and drop in.

In this example, you'd either have to aim at seven or eight o'clock and drill it with a bit more speed than normal, or you'd have to drain it by aiming just outside the cup and stroking it with less force so it will curve into the hole. If you have solid confidence in the effectiveness of your bulletproof stroke to hit the ball where you aim, you can drill putts like these with more speed because you'll believe you can make the comeback putt if necessary. However, if you feel uncomfortable about the possible comeback putt, switch to your drainable mentality and visualize a slower putt with more break.

Here is a tip for the more advanced weekend player: you can opt for *drillable* on grey zone putts that are uphill or flat and left to right breaking putts (for righties). Lean more toward *drainable* on downhill and right to left breaking putts.

In any event, it is vital to make your drill-or-drain decision early in your pre-shot routine and then to stick with it. When you are in the grey zone, either choice can be effective; so *choose one and commit fully to it.* Do not allow doubts or second guesses to intrude in your routine. If doubt or indecision creeps in as you stand over the putt, I advise you to back off, look again at the roll path from downline, and make your final decision with conviction. (I am not trying to make you the slowest player in golf history, but I do want you to build the habit of confidence in your strategy.)

Here's a summary description of how you slightly modify your routine for drainable putts:

1. Maintain the sense of deliberateness and focus you bring to every putt.
2. When you sense in your GES analysis and pre shot routine that the putt is not drillable, say, "This is a

drainable putt..." Flip the mental switch that turns on the vacuum force in the cup.

3. From downline, imagine the ball rolling the last twelve inches or so up to the hole and crossing a specific spot on the rim of the cup (ex., four o'clock) with enough speed to hit the back of the cup about half-way down. Do this at least twice.

4. Then begin at the ball and visualize the entire roll path, focusing on ball speed, and ending with the ball entering the cup as before. It is ok to pick intermediate spots the ball will cross over, but not necessary.

5. Take your normal putting stance, aligning the guide on your putter head to a spot hole-high, to the right or left of the entry point on the cup, in a casual manner.

6. Return your attention to imagining the ball rolling over the entry spot on the cup at the appropriate speed to strike the back of the cup about half way down.

7. Look at the ball and anticipate the feeling of stroking the ball gracefully along the roll path at the desired speed.

8. Make your bullet proof stroke, trusting your body to roll the ball with proper speed and path to drain into the hole.

Lag Putts

Lag putts include all putts that are not slam dunkable, drillable, or drainable. They range from, say, twelve feet on fast, steep greens, to as many as one hundred feet in length. The realistic goal of a lag putt is to leave the ball within slam dunk range for the next putt. Sure, some tour players tell us they try to make every putt, regardless of length or slope. That is fine for them, but a primary goal of bulletproof lag putting is *to avoid the dreaded three-putt*. On putts of fifteen to twenty feet, tour players routinely will make about one in five; weekend golfers will be lucky to make half that many. So, let us focus instead on lagging these longer putts into slam-dunkable - or at worst, drillable - range.

Lag putts are very similar to drainable putts. The typical lag putt requires a roll path that curves a lot more than a couple of inches, so we do not aim the putter at the cup. As with drainable putts, we rely more on *feel* than on mechanics. In fact, feel is even more important in lag putting because controlling distance is fundamentally a matter of feel, and successful lag putting is mostly about distance control.

There is one significant difference between drainable and lag putts. With lag putts, we give the ball just enough speed to fall gently over the leading edge of the cup, instead of hitting the back of the cup halfway down. We don't endeavor to hit the ball with enough speed to run past the cup on misses. We want the ball to "die at the hole."

Why is this? It is just plain easier to calibrate your stroke to die the ball at the hole than to run it eighteen inches past the hole. If your die-it-at-the hole stroke is a bit too hard or too soft, you can keep it in slam dunk range; but if you strike your carry-it-eighteen-inches-past putt a bit too hard, you'll run it out of slam dunk range. I believe this is a mistake weekend golfers make on medium to long lag putts. Thinking "never up, never in," they blow them by the hole, well outside slam dunk range. (They often compound the mistake by not giving the remaining drillable or drainable putt the attention it deserves.)

Many teachers advocate visualizing a circle with a three foot radius around the hole, and aiming for that on lag putts. This makes sense to me, provided that you try to stop the ball in the center of the circle. I realize this strategy means you will stroke putts that roll on a beautiful line only to die just an inch or two short of the cup. Instead of lamenting your misfortune, simply be happy you left yourself an easy slam dunk for your two-putt, and head to the next hole. It was a lag putt and you achieved your two-putt objective.

On greens with severe slopes, you might need to trick your body on uphill and downhill putts by picking targets that are short of or well beyond the hole. This is especially true on fast, downhill putts where it is easy to run the ball far outside the slam dunk range. In these cases, pick an intermediate spot – an imaginary cup – partway to the hole and feel that you are giving the putt just enough energy to reach that spot. On really slick downhill putts, that imaginary spot might be less than halfway to the hole. From there to the hole, the putt runs almost entirely on the force of gravity as it trickles down to the cup.

On rare occasions, you might have a very steep, uphill putt that requires you to hit to an imaginary cup a few feet past the actual hole. In general, though, you will be well served on most lag putts by vividly imagining the ball dying into the hole with its last joule of energy.

As I said in Lesson 2, the best location to determine if your putt is uphill or downhill is from the side of the target line, midway between the ball and the hole, preferably on the low side when there is significant side-slope. From there you can rotate your head to look first at the ball and then to the hole. It will be easy to see which is higher, even on combination breaking putts. If you have trouble deciding, the elevation change is probably minimal and you can play a level putt.

On long lag putts, assess your line from a ninety degree angle on the lower side to determine whether your putt is uphill or downhill.

Calibrating your stroke for accurate *distance control* on lag putting is primarily a matter of visualization and rehearsal. It takes patience and dedication to visualize the entire roll path and speed of a long lag putt, but it is a worthy endeavor. Position yourself downline from your ball on the green as soon as possible, and give yourself time to make a practice stroke and visualize the entire roll path. Two or three repetitions are ideal, time allowing. Your goal is to achieve a practice stroke that *feels* right, causing you to think "That's it!" as your imaginary ball slinks up to the cup and drops over the edge. If you are playing on unfamiliar greens, take a few seconds at the end of each hole to stroke a long lag practice putt to a specific spot before you leave the green. Within a few holes you will feel confident that your sense of speed is dialed in.

While achieving proper distance does rank higher in importance, deciphering the *correct amount of break* is another vital aspect of successful lag putting. On very long putts, you might occasionally have trouble deciding whether your putt will break right-to-left or left-to-right. If you guess wrong, the likelihood of drifting outside slam dunk range is high.

As I mentioned in Lesson 3, a helpful way to assess side-slope on long lag putts is to search for the **fall line**, the imaginary line on which a ball would roll straight into the hole with no break – basically straight uphill or downhill, depending on whether it starts from a point above or below the hole. The farther away your ball is from the fall line, the more your roll path is likely to curve on the way to the hole.

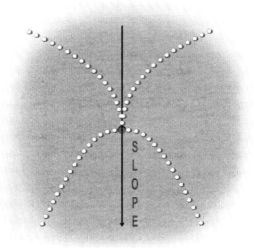

Identifying the fall line near the hole can help you assess the direction and amount of break in your putt. Putts curve towards the fall line.

Uphill roll paths always curve toward the fall line. When your ball sits to the right of your fall line, your uphill roll path will curve to the left as it approaches the hole. Conversely, when your ball lies to the left of your fall line, your uphill roll path will curve to the right. Your goal is to have your uphill putt touch the fall line at the point corresponding to the center of the cup. Steeper uphill rollpaths will curve more dramatically at the end of the journey – and more in total – than those on relatively flatter greens.

On downhill, curving putts, let your ball "die" onto the fall line above the hole and get pulled by gravity down the fall line and into the hole. On very steep, fast, downhill putts, you'll need to get the ball onto the fall line farther away from the hole. On slower, less steep downhill putts, the ball should die onto the fall line much closer to the cup.

Identifying the fall line can be highly useful in some cases, but don't trouble yourself if you find the concept confusing. Simply spend a moment looking for the imaginary line from which an uphill or downhill putt will roll straight to the hole. If you cannot identify it fairly easily, let it go and assess your putt from behind the ball using the GES List we discussed in Lesson 2.

After you decide which direction the ball will break, you need to get a feel of how much curve to allow for. While this is largely a matter of intuition, it is helpful to remember that – for any given slope and grain – putts always break more on fast greens. This holds true for both uphill and downhill putts. In other words, a thirty-foot putt that breaks three feet on a relatively slow green might break twice as much, or more, if the green is running considerably faster. This is especially dramatic when you are putting down-grain, because you have to roll the ball with even less initial velocity. On large, fast, sloping and grainy greens, pay close attention to the roll paths of each player in your group, and you'll avoid catastrophic misjudgments.

Aiming lag putts is similar to aiming drainable putts. Dave Pelz's research has demonstrated that most amateurs dramatically underestimate the amount of break in long putts, yet they somehow make a subconscious adjustment during the putting stroke to start the ball on a more appropriate line. My own observations bear this out. For this reason, I don't want you to become too fastidious about picking a precise series of intermediate targets on lag putts. Sure, you can and should pick a spot that you sense is the apex of your curving roll path and align your putter and stance more or less in that direction. Then immediately return your attention to imagining the ball completing the last several feet of its journey at a speed that lets it trickle gently over a specific spot on the circumference of the cup. Keep that image and feeling alive as you patiently stroke your long putt.

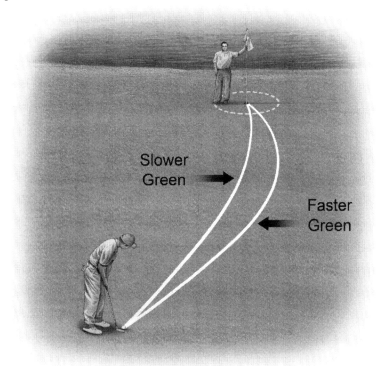

Lag your long putts into the middle of a circle with a three-foot radius around the cup, and remember that lag putts curve more on faster greens.

Although this lesson is not about the putting stroke, it is worth mentioning that the rhythm and tempo of your lag putting stroke should feel similar to that of your drillable and drainable putts. Only the length of the stroke is different. Your backstroke and follow-through strokes will be longer, and the ratio of backswing to follow-through length becomes closer to one-to-one for longer lag putts.

Curiously, the time elapsed for the stroke on longer putts is nearly identical to that for shorter putts. The putter moves faster through impact on longer strokes, which, of course, is why the ball rolls farther. However, you should not consciously think about swinging faster or hitting harder. Simply visualize the roll path and speed and maintain good rhythm and tempo on the longer stroke your body creates.

Here is a summary description of how you slightly modify your basic routine for lag putts:

1. Maintain the sense of deliberateness and focus you bring to every putt.
2. When you decide in your GES analysis and pre shot routine that your most reasonable goal is to two-putt, say, "This is a lag putt..." Flip the mental switch that turns on the vacuum force in the cup, as you do with drainable putts.
3. From downline, imagine the ball rolling the last twelve inches or so up to the hole and crossing a specific spot on the rim of the cup (ex., four o'clock), with just enough speed to trickle over the rim of the cup. Do this at least twice.

4. Starting at the ball, visualize the entire roll path, focusing on ball speed, and ending with the ball entering the cup as before. It is ok to pick intermediate spots the ball will cross over, but not necessary. If it feels good, do it.

5. While you are visualizing the ball rolling at a good speed along the path, make one or two practice swings to synch up the feel of the stroke with the desired ball speed.

6. Take your normal putting stance, aligning the guide on your putter head in a casual manner to a spot hole-high, to the right or left of the entry point on the cup, depending on the roll path. Focus on feeling where you should align the putter.

7. Return your attention to imagining the ball rolling over the entry spot on the cup at the appropriate speed to die just as it trickles into the cup.

8. Look at the ball and anticipate the feeling of stroking the ball gracefully along the roll path at the desired speed.

9. Make your bulletproof stroke, trusting your body to roll the ball with proper speed and path to drain into the hole.

One last item related to lag putting deserves a bit of discussion. What should you do when you get a dramatically different feeling about the appropriate roll path when you stand over the ball, compared to when you assessed it from your down line view? For example, perhaps you decide your thirty foot lag putt would break about two feet from right to left, yet, after you take your putting stance, you suddenly feel the putt is actually going to break about the same amount from left to right. If you pick the wrong option, you could easily leave the putt outside slam dunk or even drillable range.

I have two suggestions. Initially at least, trust your down-line read and ignore the reassessment generated from your putting stance. I say this because your binocular vision has a much better chance of reading the break accurately from down line than it does while you are bent over the ball and rotating your head in your putting stance. That said, my second suggestion is to make a mental note each time this situation arises and keep track of which assessment proves correct. After a handful of occurrences, you should be able to put this conflict to rest and know which read to trust in your own game.

Lesson 5 - Practice and On-course Putting Tips

"Practice putting more than anything, absolutely anything."
-Matthew Fitzpatrick, 2013 US Amateur Champion

*"About all there is to putting is to keep your head steady
and the face of your putter square to the direction as you
stroke the ball."*
-Tommy Armour, *Classic Golf Tips*

I have to smile and shake my head as I consider
Tommy Armour's summary analysis of putting. If it were
that simple for all of us, there certainly would be no need
for putting practice. Perhaps that attitude is why many
weekend golfers shun putting practice, preferring instead
to sneak onto the course for a few holes or to work on
their full swings by beating balls at the range.

Who can blame them? Putting practice seems boring
and unproductive compared to grinding on your full
swing. The dirty little secret is this: full swing practice
delivers little if any sustainable improvement in the
scores of weekend players, because the golf swing is a
complex motor pattern that is difficult to reprogram. As
we all have experienced, seemingly successful swing
changes achieved during a productive practice session
often evaporate inexplicably before the next outing.

On the other hand, putting practice can lower your
scores more quickly than any other endeavor. For this
reason – and despite the fact that few golfers want to

practice putting, let alone read about the topic – I'll offer a handful of straightforward suggestions on how to make the most of the precious few minutes you do devote to putting practice.

There are four opportunities to practice putting:

1. Around your home or office
2. When you practice the rest of your game
3. Before teeing off for a round of golf
4. During a round of golf.

Around the Home and Office

As I mentioned previously, the Bulletproof Putting System requires you to reliably stroke a relatively short, straight putt at an appropriate speed along your intended line. You'll agree that this is not difficult, provided you follow my suggestions on set up and stroke in Lesson 1. Nevertheless, it does take practice to make it automatic and to convince yourself that, yes, you are an expert at drilling straight putts into the heart of the cup.

An easy way to achieve this level of skill and confidence is to practice for just a few minutes each day at home or in your office. Two to five minutes a day are plenty. In fact, it is valuable to putt for just one minute, several times a day. I recommend a practice rug such as the *SKLZ-Accelerator* or simply a long ruler or piece of tape to train your stroke and a coin or cup to serve as a target. Your goals should be 1) to convince yourself you can aim and stroke your putter consistently along a straight line for a few inches on either side of the ball, 2) to ingrain your bulletproof putting routines for slam dunk and drillable putts, and 3) to stroke the ball to your target at an appropriate speed.

Since this indoor practice focuses on slam dunk and drillable putts, be sure to draw a stripe on the ball and align it to your intended target. This takes time to line up every time and might seem utterly unnecessary, but it is vital that you build a habit you can trust on the golf course when the pressure is on. Mastering the alignment of the stripe to the target at home will eliminate the debilitating FUD of standing over a drillable putt for par and wondering, "Is that stripe really lined up correctly?"

Indoor practice is the only venue in which I recommend performing many repetitions of the same putt line and length because these repetitions are needed to train and ingrain your bulletproof putting stroke. This is the vital half of your battle to master putting. When you move to the outdoor practice venues, you'll simply rely on your bulletproof stroke as you work on your GES analysis, your preshot and inshot routines, your aggressive visualization, and your confidence.

Commit today to finding a spare putter, a couple of balls, an alignment guide and a target, and to spending at least a couple of minutes every day grooving your bulletproof stroke. You might set a daily goal of making ten in a row from a given distance. Ideally, the putter should be a similar design to your on-course putter, but this is not at all necessary. You can use virtually any putter to build a repeatable, mechanical, drillable putting stroke. Start today!

When You Practice the Rest of Your Game

Even though putting consumes at least forty percent of our shots, very few weekend golfers are willing to devote more than ten percent of their practice time to putting. This implies that a typical golfer who beats balls on the range for one hour *might* stop at the putting green for five to ten minutes. I ask you to commit to at least that amount of putting practice whenever possible. Every time your golf practice takes you anywhere near a putting green, stop for at least five minutes of putting practice.

If you can invest only five minutes, spend it all on drillable putts. These are the most important putts to master. Drop a half-dozen balls in a circle three to six feet in diameter around one hole on a relatively flat part of the practice green, and work your way around the circle. Take the little flag stick out of the hole, so you can visualize the ball striking the back of the cup. Go through your drillable routine, line up the stripe, take your stance and drill each putt with the appropriate speed to strike the back of the cup one to two inches from the top. Focus on repeating your routine with militaristic efficiency. Keep your mind on your task and do not let it wander. Those will be five well-spent minutes.

If you can invest ten minutes, spend the first five on drillable putts and the last five on lag putts. With two to four balls, find the farthest hole on the practice green and aim for that. Do *not* just step up and whack the ball with little or no forethought. Instead, perform your lag putting routine as if you were on the course. Visualize the roll path, rehearse the length of stroke, and imagine the speed of the putt. Awaken your sense of feel. After you stroke the first putt, repeat the process for a second time, making any adjustments necessary in aim and stroke. Then, regardless of the outcomes of the first two putts, pick a different, distant hole and begin your lag putt routine again. Do not bother putting out; simply collect your balls and hit some more lag putts of varying distances and slopes. Your goal is to lag into slam dunk or, at worst, drillable range, but there is no time or need to putt out. Spend your second five minutes refining your routine and *feel* for lag putting.

If you have fifteen minutes to invest, spend your final five minutes on drainable putts. Your sense of feel should have been awakened during your lag putting practice, and now you can enjoy the challenge of finessing a few breaking putts into the cup. Again drop your balls in a circle around a cup, but this time select a more hilly part of the practice green and make the putts a bit longer, say five to eight feet in length. Rather than simply hitting each putt mindlessly, treat each putt as if it were needed for par, and go through your drainable putt routine. There is great value to be gained from practicing all elements in your routine, taking time to kinesthetically "call forth" the *anticipated feeling* of sending the upcoming putt curving into the hole at the perfect speed.

On those rare occasions when you can invest another fifteen minutes or so, I recommend playing a game of Eleven, either by yourself or against another player (If you play alone, you'll play two balls.). The goal of the game, which is a bit like horseshoes, is to be the first to accumulate eleven points. One player selects a hole and putts toward it. The second player follows. If player one sinks the first putt, he gets three points. In the unlikely event the second player also sinks his first putt, he gets six points and the first player forfeits his three. If neither player sinks the initial putt, the ball closest to the hole scores one point, regardless of how close or far from the hole it rests. Both players then putt out, and a missed putt scores minus one point. As you can see, a player who three-putts a lot will end up in negative numbers. I like this game because it encourages you to lag long putts up close and to avoid three putting. It also creates pressure on short putts. The game of Eleven helps you practice all four putts – lag, drainable, drillable, and slam dunk – under realistic conditions. It is also highly addictive.

Practice during a Round of Golf

When you arrive at the course for a round of golf, plan to spend at least five minutes on the practice green before teeing off. I believe this simple investment can save you two to three shots a round. Don't bother idly stroking fifteen and twenty footers while chatting with your pals. You won't make a very high percentage. Instead, take two or three balls and start by hitting a handful of successful slam dunks. Then switch to stroking a few very long lag putts. Stay with this until you gain confidence that you have calibrated your stroke to the speed of the greens and you can lag the ball reasonably close from anywhere on the green. Time allowing, hit just a handful of drainable putts from five to eight feet in length, and finish off with a half dozen drillable putts from four to six feet. Be sure to line up your stripe and follow your routine. In this process, you rehearse all the important putts that can save you strokes on the course.

You will notice I do not advocate practicing putts of ten to twenty feet in length during your pre-round warm up, even though that is precisely what many weekend golfers do. If you calibrate your stroke for long lag putts, distance control on these intermediate putts will be a no brainer. If you hit a few drainable putts, your feel for curving roll paths will be awakened enough to transfer to slightly longer putts. Some readers might protest, "Hey, Mike, my chipping is so lousy that I rarely leave myself a putt shorter than ten feet." If that's the case, spend more time working on your chipping skill and forget about practicing low percentage putts.

During the round, you have good opportunities to practice. At a minimum, make it a habit to hit one very long putt at the conclusion of each hole. Aim toward a portion of the green near your bag on the way to the next tee. Your goal is to keep your stroke calibrated for very long lag putts. As the round progresses, your lag putting will get sharper and sharper, and even the longest putts on the course won't worry you.

Your second opportunity, depending on the flow of play, is to hit a drainable or drillable putt at the conclusion of each hole, before or after placing the flag in the cup. It might be tempting, but don't bother trying to sink the fifteen footer you just missed. Instead, pick an interesting putt of five feet or less and knock it into the hole. The purpose of this is to reduce anxiety and FUD around makeable putts. The more you make, the better you'll feel.

Let me repeat my admonition NOT to spend your precious practice time working on putts of fifteen to twenty-five feet in length, despite the fact that you probably face several or more of these every round. If you have lots of time to practice, feel free to include some of these hybrid lag-drainable putts. On the other hand, assuming you are a weekend player with limited practice time, don't spend much if any time in this low percentage zone. On average, the best players in the world make less than one in five putts from fifteen to twenty feet, which suggests that half of them do even worse. You are unlikely to experience greater success, which is not good for your confidence.

I recommend investing your practice time where the payoffs will be the greatest: learning to lag long putts into a makeable range and getting bulletproof at sinking drillable and drainable putts inside an eight foot radius. Besides, both of these skills will carry over to improve your success in the low percentage zone.

Parting Shots

"Nonchalant putts count the same as chalant putts."
-Henry Beard

Let's review the goals of this book as presented in its Introduction. I offered you a system for increasing one-putts and reducing three-putts that focused on two primary goals: sinking more putts of eight feet or less and lagging longer putts into your Slam Dunk Zone to avoid three putting. To achieve these goals, we invested in five lessons, each with a definite purpose:

Lesson 1: Building a simple, repeatable, dependable putting stroke. If you devote a little time every day to home practice of the basic pendulum stroke described, I am sure you will achieve this objective within a few weeks.

Lesson 2: Developing curiosity and imagination about "roll-path." Reading greens is a lifelong challenge that always leaves room for improvement. Attention, curiosity, active imagination, and patience are vital personal traits. The GES List system of reading greens adds elements of discipline and structure to this largely intuitive endeavor. Remember, it is possible to imagine every putt traversing its roll path into the heart of the cup. It gets easier with practice.

Lesson 3: Ingraining your bulletproof pre-shot and in-shot routines. You cannot be bulletproof without a routine! If you have not worked on this yet, please make it a priority because it is a powerful antidote to FUD. Watch tour players and you will agree that the majority follow their established routines on every putt. Work on your routine during practice sessions so you won't have to worry about it on the course. For the first week or two, refer to a little index card with a list of your steps. Pretty soon, you will just do it.

Lesson 4: Learning strategies for the four types of putts: slam dunk, drillable, drainable, and lag. The *drillable* versus *drainable* dichotomy is perhaps the most useful aspect of bulletproof putting. The other two types of putts, slam dunks and lag putts, relate closely to drillable and drainable putts, respectively. The process of deciding which type of putt you are facing forces you to imagine intently the roll path of the ball as it approaches and enters the cup. This visualization increases your confidence that the putt is makeable and you know how it must be made. Committing fully to either a *mechanistic* drillable mentality or a *feel-heightened* drainable mentality sends important information to your body about the required stroke. Then you initiate the appropriate routine and wait with Zen-like patience as your body makes the stroke.

Lesson 5: Utilizing your precious practice and warm up time to best advantage. No one expects you to spend the appropriate percentage of your practice time on putting, but you can be smart about how you use the time you allocate. Indoor practice helps you groove your bulletproof putting stroke and ingrain your-stance and stroke routines. Outdoor practice helps you master your GES List analysis, ingrain your preshot routine, and improve your ability to execute each of the four types of putts. When time is tight, focus on drillable putts and long lag putts. With more time available, add drainable putts and competitive games of Eleven.

Using these lessons as a checklist, how do you feel about your achievement in each of them? If you have a sense of mastery of each lesson, you surely are enjoying the feeling of bulletproof confidence that overrides fear, uncertainty, and doubt. You might even be excited about facing tricky putts such as downhill sliders or long, double-breaking putts.

If your putting has not improved to your satisfaction, you can use the checklist to determine which of the elements of the bulletproof system are not yet fully functional in your game. Here are a few guidelines:

- If you miss a lot of slam dunks and drillable putts, your alignment and stroke are not bulletproof. Refer to Lesson 1.
- If your lag and drainable putts are disappointing, your understanding of roll path might be weak, or your imagination might be underutilized. Refer to Lessons 2 and 4.
- If you putt consistently better during practice than on the course, your routine is leaky and the pressure is getting to you. Refer to Lesson 3.
- If your putting deteriorates as the round progresses, you are losing your feel and confidence. Refer to Lessons 4 and 5.

Analyzing Your Putting

Are you a data wonk who tracks your shot making stats and records your number of putts per hole and per round? This is fun, but it gives you little in the way of actionable information to improve your putting. For those readers having the time and interest in analyzing their on-course putting in more detail, I concocted a little scoring sheet to help you understand how you perform on various types of putts. In a nutshell, you can track the type of putt you face, the slope, the break, and the result, and the reason for your misses. It is an Excel spreadsheet you can *download* (http://goo.gl/YLRcq5), print out, and carry with you on the golf course. By examining a few rounds of putts in this manner, you might be able to identify certain proclivities, such as frequently missing uphill, left-to-right breaking putts on the left side of the hole because of misreads or mis-strokes. If you are familiar with Excel, you can sort selected columns, such as Misread, to see which types of putts you most frequently misread. Of course, I do not expect the typical weekend golf to bother with such recordkeeping, but I hope it will prove useful to a few analytical minds.

Here is an example of three holes filled in, with a quickie analysis. Have a look and see if you can decipher how this golfer putted on her first three holes.

Hole	Type				Length	Slope			Break			Result					Why?	
1	L	DL	DN	SD	40	Up	Dn	Lvl	L-R	R-L	ST	Gd	Sh	Lg	Hi	Lo	Rd	Str
1	L	DL	DN	SD	6	Up	Dn	Lvl	L-R	R-L	ST	Gd	Sh	Lg	Hi	Lo	Rd	Str
2	L	DL	DN	SD	20	Up	Dn	Lvl	L-R	R-L	ST	Gd	Sh	Lg	Hi	Lo	Rd	Str
2	L	DL	DN	SD	2	Up	Dn	Lvl	L-R	R-L	ST	Gd	Sh	Lg	Hi	Lo	Rd	Str
3	L	DL	DN	SD	7	Up	Dn	Lvl	L-R	R-L	ST	Gd	Sh	Lg	Hi	Lo	Rd	Str

Key

Type: L=lag; DL=drillable; DN=drainable; S=slam dunk

Slope: Up=uphill; Dn=downhill; Lvl=level

Break: L-R=left-to-right; R-L=left-to-right; ST=straight

Result: Gd=good; SH=miss short; LG=miss long; Hi=miss high; Lo=miss low

Why (missed): Rd=misread; Str=mis-stroke

On hole one, the player lagged her forty-foot, uphill, right-to-left breaking putt short of and below the hole because of a mis-read. She followed up by sinking her drillable six-foot, uphill, straight putt. On hole two, she lagged her twenty-foot downhill, left-to-right putt to within two feet short of the hole. Her result for this putt shows both "good" and "short," because she achieved her goal of leaving her lag putt within slam dunk range. She sunk her two-foot, level, slam dunk putt. On the third hole, she chipped to within seven feet, leaving a drainable, downhill, right-to-left putt. She made the putt, but her success was due to both a misread and a mis-hit (which sometimes happens!). As you can see, this little sheet tells you a lot about your putting results. I suggest trying it for one or two rounds and seeing what you discover about yourself.

Hole	Type				Length	Slope			Break			Result					Why?	
	L	DL	DN	SD		Up	Dn	Lvl	L-R	R-L	ST	Gd	Sh	Lg	Hi	Lo	Rd	Str
	L	DL	DN	SD		Up	Dn	Lvl	L-R	R-L	ST	Gd	Sh	Lg	Hi	Lo	Rd	Str
	L	DL	DN	SD		Up	Dn	Lvl	L-R	R-L	ST	Gd	Sh	Lg	Hi	Lo	Rd	Str
	L	DL	DN	SD		Up	Dn	Lvl	L-R	R-L	ST	Gd	Sh	Lg	Hi	Lo	Rd	Str
	L	DL	DN	SD		Up	Dn	Lvl	L-R	R-L	ST	Gd	Sh	Lg	Hi	Lo	Rd	Str
	L	DL	DN	SD		Up	Dn	Lvl	L-R	R-L	ST	Gd	Sh	Lg	Hi	Lo	Rd	Str
	L	DL	DN	SD		Up	Dn	Lvl	L-R	R-L	ST	Gd	Sh	Lg	Hi	Lo	Rd	Str
	L	DL	DN	SD		Up	Dn	Lvl	L-R	R-L	ST	Gd	Sh	Lg	Hi	Lo	Rd	Str
	L	DL	DN	SD		Up	Dn	Lvl	L-R	R-L	ST	Gd	Sh	Lg	Hi	Lo	Rd	Str
	L	DL	DN	SD		Up	Dn	Lvl	L-R	R-L	ST	Gd	Sh	Lg	Hi	Lo	Rd	Str
	L	DL	DN	SD		Up	Dn	Lvl	L-R	R-L	ST	Gd	Sh	Lg	Hi	Lo	Rd	Str
	L	DL	DN	SD		Up	Dn	Lvl	L-R	R-L	ST	Gd	Sh	Lg	Hi	Lo	Rd	Str
	L	DL	DN	SD		Up	Dn	Lvl	L-R	R-L	ST	Gd	Sh	Lg	Hi	Lo	Rd	Str
	L	DL	DN	SD		Up	Dn	Lvl	L-R	R-L	ST	Gd	Sh	Lg	Hi	Lo	Rd	Str
	L	DL	DN	SD		Up	Dn	Lvl	L-R	R-L	ST	Gd	Sh	Lg	Hi	Lo	Rd	Str
	L	DL	DN	SD		Up	Dn	Lvl	L-R	R-L	ST	Gd	Sh	Lg	Hi	Lo	Rd	Str
	L	DL	DN	SD		Up	Dn	Lvl	L-R	R-L	ST	Gd	Sh	Lg	Hi	Lo	Rd	Str
	L	DL	DN	SD		Up	Dn	Lvl	L-R	R-L	ST	Gd	Sh	Lg	Hi	Lo	Rd	Str
	L	DL	DN	SD		Up	Dn	Lvl	L-R	R-L	ST	Gd	Sh	Lg	Hi	Lo	Rd	Str
	L	DL	DN	SD		Up	Dn	Lvl	L-R	R-L	ST	Gd	Sh	Lg	Hi	Lo	Rd	Str
	L	DL	DN	SD		Up	Dn	Lvl	L-R	R-L	ST	Gd	Sh	Lg	Hi	Lo	Rd	Str
	L	DL	DN	SD		Up	Dn	Lvl	L-R	R-L	ST	Gd	Sh	Lg	Hi	Lo	Rd	Str
	L	DL	DN	SD		Up	Dn	Lvl	L-R	R-L	ST	Gd	Sh	Lg	Hi	Lo	Rd	Str
	L	DL	DN	SD		Up	Dn	Lvl	L-R	R-L	ST	Gd	Sh	Lg	Hi	Lo	Rd	Str
	L	DL	DN	SD		Up	Dn	Lvl	L-R	R-L	ST	Gd	Sh	Lg	Hi	Lo	Rd	Str
	L	DL	DN	SD		Up	Dn	Lvl	L-R	R-L	ST	Gd	Sh	Lg	Hi	Lo	Rd	Str
	L	DL	DN	SD		Up	Dn	Lvl	L-R	R-L	ST	Gd	Sh	Lg	Hi	Lo	Rd	Str
	L	DL	DN	SD		Up	Dn	Lvl	L-R	R-L	ST	Gd	Sh	Lg	Hi	Lo	Rd	Str
	L	DL	DN	SD		Up	Dn	Lvl	L-R	R-L	ST	Gd	Sh	Lg	Hi	Lo	Rd	Str
	L	DL	DN	SD		Up	Dn	Lvl	L-R	R-L	ST	Gd	Sh	Lg	Hi	Lo	Rd	Str
	L	DL	DN	SD		Up	Dn	Lvl	L-R	R-L	ST	Gd	Sh	Lg	Hi	Lo	Rd	Str
	L	DL	DN	SD		Up	Dn	Lvl	L-R	R-L	ST	Gd	Sh	Lg	Hi	Lo	Rd	Str
	L	DL	DN	SD		Up	Dn	Lvl	L-R	R-L	ST	Gd	Sh	Lg	Hi	Lo	Rd	Str
	L	DL	DN	SD		Up	Dn	Lvl	L-R	R-L	ST	Gd	Sh	Lg	Hi	Lo	Rd	Str

Key

Type: L=lag; DL=drillable; DN=drainable; S=slam dunk

Slope: Up=uphill; Dn=downhill; Lvl=level

Break: L-R=left-to-right; R-L=left-to-right; ST=straight

Result: Gd=good; SH=miss short; LG=miss long; Hi=miss high; Lo=miss lo

Why (missed): Rd=misread; Str=mis-stroke

This Worked for Me

My own putting improved as a result of writing this book. Four concepts have been especially useful, so I offer them as a brief summary of the bulletproof putting system.

- I improved my short putting significantly by convincing myself I can aim and stroke my putter online for five inches on each side of the ball. When facing a makeable straight putt, I can easily imagine my at-home practice of moving the putter back-and-through above a straight line. This mental certainty replaces negative thoughts with patience and positive expectancy.
- My confidence also improved from the process of adding to every preshot routine my proactive decision between *drillable* and *drainable* mindsets. (Recall that slam dunks are also drillable and lag putts are also drainable, so every putt is either drillable or drainable.) While initially this process caused some consternation, especially on putts in the five to eight foot range, a surge of commitment and confidence inevitably follows the moment of decision, when I say, "This is *drillable*," or "This is *drainable*."
- Aggressive visualization is helpful on every putt. I am much more diligent about visualizing the roll path of the ball, with special focus the last twelve inches where the ball crosses the ideal point on the

circumference of the cup. This is useful even on the longest lag putts.

- A major key to success is to complete the visualization process by imagining the ball *hitting the back of the cup at the desired distance below the surface*. This is a powerful, final, mental picture to hold as you start your stroke.

Remember, you *can* and *must* vividly imagine every putt rolling into the cup at the appropriate speed.

I wish you the greatest success!

Bibliography

Pelz, D. and J. Frank. *Dave Pelz's Putting Bible*, New York: Doubleday, 2000. *(http://goo.gl/bkC3FC)*

Editors, Golf Magazine. *The Best Putting Instruction Book Ever*. New York: Time Home Entertainment, 2010 *(http://goo.gl/rEkpyS)*

Farnsworth, Craig. *The Putting Prescription: The Putt Doctor's Proven Method for a Better Stroke*, New York: Wiley, 2009. *(http://goo.gl/SvNro3)*

Nicklaus, Jack. *Golf My Way*, New York: Simon & Schuster, 1974 *(http://goo.gl/ru26nc)*

Stockton, Dave. *Dave Stockton's Putt to Win*, New York: Simon & Schuster. 1996 *(http://goo.gl/DsNK3V)*

Stockton, D. and M. Rudy. *Unconscious Putting: Dave Stockton's Guide to Unlocking Your Signature Stroke*, New York: Gotham, 2011 *(http://goo.gl/zIUkiY)*

Jones, Robert Tyre. *Bobby Jones on Golf,* New York, Main Street Books, 1966 *(http://goo.gl/DbWfqm)*

Floyd, Raymond. *The Elements of Scoring: A Master's Guide to the Art of Scoring Your Best When You're Not Playing Your Best*, New York: Simon & Schuster, 2000 *(http://goo.gl/nt3FZD)*

Woods, Tiger. *How I Play Golf*, New York: Grand Central Publishing, 2001. *(http://goo.gl/Jh2409)*

Paul Runyan. *The Short Way to Lower Scoring.* New York: Simon & Schuster. 1982. (*http://goo.gl/7nlcFw*)

Parent, Joseph. *How to Make Every Putt: The Secret to Winning Golf's Game Within the Game*, New York: Gotham, 2011. (*http://goo.gl/6ERybD*)

McTeigue, Michael. *The Keys to the Effortless Golf Swing - Curing Your Hit Impulse in Seven Simple Lessons*, New York: Atheneum, 1985. (*http://goo.gl/GLXbwN*)

About the Author

As a member of the U.S. Professional Golfers' Association (PGA), Michael McTeigue conducted thousands of golf lessons as assistant golf professional at Bel Air Country Club, teaching professional at Riviera Country Club, and head golf professional at Palos Verdes Golf Club.

Michael was voted the 1995 Teacher of the Year for the Northern California Section of the PGA. He served as a faculty member in the PGA's Golf Professional Training Program and as an instructor in the PGA's Professional Training and Development Seminar Program. He has authored numerous instruction articles for publications such as GOLF Magazine, Golf Digest, and Senior Golfer. His first golf instruction book, *The Keys to the Effortless Golf Swing,* has been a popular seller on Amazon.com for many years.

Michael graduated Phi Beta Kappa from UCLA with a degree in Psychology, and he received his MBA from Stanford University's Graduate School of Business. He resides in San Mateo, CA with his wife and two daughters.

Made in the USA
Columbia, SC
29 April 2021